'Draper takes the vogue for mindfulness to a deeper level: soulfulness.'

Oliver James, psychologist and
bestselling author of *Affluenza*

'*Soulfulness* might seem like yet another book on mindfulness, but it is actually quite radical. It takes the good things of that practice and adds some salt and light to the mix. It seeks to wake us up, wherever we are on our spiritual journey.'

Church Times

'Using consistently thoughtful and dynamic writing, Draper takes us on a journey of discovery to the heart of who we are as individuals and how we can live life to the full. This is a book to dwell on rather than devour, as it offers practical exercises to help move us towards soulfulness in our own lives. We could all do with picking up this book. After all, it's in waking up to our souls that we really find out what it means to live.'

Christianity magazine

'Reading Brian Draper's new book *Soulfulness* is like coming home, but realizing home is even more spacious than you had imagined. This is mindfulness at its most simple and profound, embodied, relational, brimming with ethical attentiveness. The Christian way of life it

outlines is deeply attentive to the things of God, and in
so doing reveals a path of joy.'

The Baptist Times

'Simple and beautiful, an inspirational book for all. The
main point of this moving and thought-provoking book
is to help us become more fully alive, more acutely
aware and to appreciate the present moment.'

The Irish Catholic

Soulfulness

Deepening the Mindful Life

BRIAN DRAPER

HODDER

First published in Great Britain in 2016 by Hodder & Stoughton
An Hachette UK company

This paperback edition first published in 2017

5

Copyright © Brian Draper, 2016

A CIP catalogue record for this title is available from the British Library

ISBN 978 1 473 63075 8
eBook ISBN 978 1 473 63076 5

Typeset in Sabon LT by Hewer Text UK Ltd, Edinburgh
Printed and bound in the UK by Clays Ltd, Elcograf S.p.A.

Hodder & Stoughton policy is to use papers that are natural, renewable and recyclable products and made from wood grown in sustainable forests. The logging and manufacturing processes are expected to conform to the environmental regulations of the country of origin.

Hodder & Stoughton Ltd
Carmelite House
50 Victoria Embankment
London EC4Y 0DZ

www.hodderfaith.com

To Peggy, a radiant soul

Contents

Introduction   1

Part 1:
What's right with mindfulness?
An appreciative enquiry

1 How do you drink your tea?   11
2 How mindful practice can
   prepare us for the soulful life   20
3 Consciousness discipline –
   and the way the brain takes us deeper   26
4 Turning 'time out' into 'time in'   35

INTERLUDE: Are you ready for adventure?   49

Part 2:
Reaching in for soul: awakening
to our unique, inner aliveness

5 Awake, my soul!   59
6 Sensing the soulful life   79
7 Meeting your self, as if for the first time   86
8 Sharpening the focus on our
   uniqueness – some questions to ponder   103

Part 3:

Reaching out with soul: reconnecting lovingly with all parts of life

9   Soul friendship   113
10 Connecting with God   120
11 To breathe the larger air:
    nature and the human soul   126
12 The space between us   145

Part 4:

Living with soul: giving flesh-and-blood expression to the soulful life

13 Fleshing out our unique, inner aliveness   155
14 *Hygge* – a warm and soulful
    embrace of the whole of life   161
15 Peace, wholeness and embracing paradox   174
16 Finding a soulful rhythm
    as natural as breathing   189
17 Soulful expression through our life's work   209
18 Let the soul take the lead   228

Epilogue: It is well with my soul   237
If you were to do one thing   241
A reminder of the exercises and
suggestions contained within this book   245
Acknowledgements   253
Notes   255

'We sense that something is missing in our lives and search the world for it, not understanding that what is missing is us.'

Parker J. Palmer

Introduction

Today I went for a run, and reached as far as a nature reserve, when, from out of the blue, the skies blackened, and hail and rain started to lash down. This wasn't the plan! As I looped back along a path that skirted the water meadows, however, the sun suddenly flooded through the falling rain once more, and above the reeds there arched the most vivid double rainbow. It stopped me in my tracks, stirred my soul, and I tried to take it in. In that moment, I felt reconnected to nature and to God; I was lifted out of my petty grievances with the world, and I felt blessed.

Yet no sooner had it appeared, and I was caught up in this reverie, than it began to fade to nothing, and was gone.

We can experience many special and unexpected moments like this; many moments of mini-awakening. Yet so often, we don't quite know what to do with them, or how to capitalise on that fleeting yet tangible sense of goodness they bring. They speak to us in the moment of *more* – of a deeper connection to be made with life, somehow – yet all too often, we run home with a head full of distractions, and launch straight back into busyness-as-usual, and they disappear, like the rainbow, to nothing.

*　　*　　*

For some time, I've been wanting to write a book that joins some of the most accessible parts of mindfulness – because it's so straightforwardly and practically helpful – with what I'm increasingly excited about: living with soul!

Mindfulness has helped me hugely: to wake up more vividly to the present moment, for example (such a precious gift in itself!), and to stay calm(er) in the face of a crisis. It helps me now to be more attentive and present to others, and to live more intentionally, and less reactively, while remaining open to the possibilities of life. More than anything, it has helped me to recognise the insecure voice of my ego, which so often wants to control life with a vice-like grip, and to compete self-ishly, and to make endless and dissatisfying comparisons with others. I've found that some of the simplest, most common-sense techniques of mindfulness have helped me to learn more about my own Christian faith, and in particular how the ego-driven 'false sense of self' can mask the true. It's unearthed for me some of the spiritual treasures that so often end up buried beneath the soulless dogma of organised religion. So in Part 1 of this book, I make an appreciative enquiry into the techniques and benefits of mindfulness.

But I'm also passionately convinced that there is more to each of us than a calmed mind alone – albeit this is a crucial place to start. And that is where *soulfulness* comes in. Mindfulness can take us to a place of peace, and poise, beyond the stresses and distractions of contemporary life, but here we find ourselves on a tantalising threshold – the threshold of soul – just as we do when we catch sight of a rainbow. But then what? What do we *do* with this?

I love the word 'soul' – it has a rich, warm and inviting connotation for me – and I'd love to step deeper, with you, into the space that 'soulfulness' opens up. It's a space, I believe, in which we can discover more of our own uniqueness and express this lovingly and purposefully through our actions. I don't want to be stuck in a soulless rut. I want to find the soulful groove, learn to live with energy and creativity, and in the process become a positive, engaging part of the solution at a troubled time! Why ever not?

So we'll ask how we can press further in, instead of pulling ourselves back into the world of ego once more. How can we step across that soulful threshold? What is soul like? How does it connect us all, what kind of space does it open, and what could a soulful life look like, when it finds expression uniquely through each of us?

It's almost impossible, of course, to pin soul down, so this is more of an artful exploration than a scientific thesis (though we'll touch on one or two fascinating insights from neuroscience along the way). But I will describe soul, for the purposes of this book, as an 'inner aliveness' that is truly unique to each of us.

In Part 2, then, I will ask how we can learn to reach inwards, to become better acquainted with the presence of our soul, and to become more intentional about welcoming and befriending it, so that we come to understand more of who we are, as a result, and the nature of our own uniqueness. (For we are all unique, despite the roles we play, and the masks we wear, and the personas we adopt.)

By reaching in for soul, we also find ourselves reaching out, *through* soul, to the world around us. Soul (re)connects us powerfully to so much more, including to other people, to God, to nature and to culture. That's what we'll explore in Part 3: how soul reconnects us, lovingly, and brings us back to life.

Finally, Part 4 asks what the soulful life looks like when we give full outward expression to our unique, inner aliveness. For this is the thing: soulfulness is not about floating off on a spiritual cloud, to a magical place far removed from our day-to-day reality. Instead, it's a down-to-earth, flesh-and-blood way to embrace, and transform, our world. How can we establish a more soulful rhythm, beyond survival and burnout? How can we learn to welcome life in its fullness, instead of trying to escape so much of it? What does soulful work look like?

I'm sure we all play our part, from time to time, in creating a soul*less* world, so what can we do to initiate a far more inspiring – more soul*ful* – example within the world around us?

If you would love to cultivate a positive difference, in your own life as well as in the life of your family and friends, your work or business, your community and, wider still, your world, then the most achievable, positive, sustainable and joyful way to do it – I believe, I really do – is to do it with soul.

The invitation does, however, come at a price. It is not a selfish, individualist pursuit. Soulfulness will not necessarily make you rich or even successful in the eyes of the culture we have fashioned for ourselves.

As Jesus, whom I follow, once put it: 'For what does it profit [anyone] to gain the whole world and forfeit their soul?' Perhaps we might add, as we set off into this adventure, 'And what might it cost to retrieve it?'

A little more about my own spirituality

I'm passionate about making vibrant connections between everyday life and the Christian faith that lies at the heart of all I am and do. But if you've ever heard me on BBC Radio 4's *Thought for the Day*, or read my other books, you'll know that I seek to make those connections in a way that avoids too much talk of religion, while maintaining the integrity and distinctiveness of my own spirituality.

In fact, my life's work has been about finding ways to explore and express this dynamic relationship between life and faith for *myself* – but in a way that touches others in the process. So I am not seeking to convert or persuade you. Instead, when I'm making reference to the Bible and Christianity in the pages that follow, I'm 'showing my working', as my mathematics teacher used to instruct me.

So this is not a book about belief. Instead, it asks: How can I live with soul?

My mind turns to a lady who has become a dear friend of mine: Peggy. She's just turned ninety-six years young, and is blessed with the kind of health and energy that means you'd probably think she was seventy if you met her. Peggy has been on some of my retreats, and comes along to an evening called Hush that I run at my local Anglican church. It's a simple hour, once a month, in which a number of us sit quietly within the 'space', and do little else. We may listen to a piece of music, or consider a seasonal theme ... but the idea is to find a place of stripped-back stillness in which we can catch our breath, and slow down, and become aware again of the 'presence' behind life – which I would call the presence of God – that was there all along, if we did but stop to notice it.

Peggy is an artist, who was put off religion in her childhood – she was sent to an overbearingly strict religious school and never quite got over it. Yet she has always been aware of, and appreciated, the spiritual nature of life, and was ever hopeful that she might one day find a 'home' for it.

Within that distinctly Christian, yet open, inclusive and spacious setting of Hush, Peggy at last found somewhere to explore and express her spirituality. She does this alongside people who may have attended church for decades, but who share Peggy's desire to connect with God and life in deep, creative and compelling ways, and that avoid being overbearingly religious.

I'd love you to see this book, too, as a soulful space in which you are most welcome, without hint of duress, to enter, and to catch your breath, and to be still . . . and to reconnect with 'life in its fullness', as Jesus once put it. Nothing more, but hopefully nothing less.

Thank you for joining me.

Part 1
What's right with mindfulness? An appreciative enquiry

1

How do you drink your tea?

The great strength of mindfulness lies in its simplicity, clarity and effectiveness. We'll touch on definitions shortly, but a helpful place to start is with its opposite. So ask yourself this: when was the last time you did something *mindlessly*?

Perhaps it was the way you ate breakfast this morning. It might have been a mad rush to get out of the door for work, or to get children ready for school or nursery. Perhaps you weren't quite as hurried, but you found yourself tuning in, instead, to the morning news on the radio and getting lost in thought, or worrying about the day ahead.

The chances are, like so many of us, you hardly noticed what you were eating, let alone how you were eating it. What did your food taste like?

Even before that, how did you rise from bed? The alarm clock might have been an unholy shock to the system, and perhaps you shot up and out, full of adrenaline, fearing you were behind before you'd even begun. Or you might have felt so dead to the world that it was a struggle to move a muscle. Either way, it's possible, or dare I say probable, that while you awoke physically (in the end!), you didn't necessarily start the day fully awake to life itself – to the great gift of 'being here' that is given to us, new every morning, if we are willing to receive it.

How about the last cup of tea you made yourself, or the coffee you bought 'to go'? Did you feel its warmth as you drank it and moved on? Were you able to savour it?

We perform many of the day's routines, rituals and tasks so automatically that it's easy to live much of our life 'mindlessly'. And mindless doesn't just mean marching through our days like zombies, unthinkingly (although we often do); an even greater challenge is that we can find it almost impossible to *stop* thinking – so that our restless and often anxious minds end up pulling us back into the past (as we re-live events, over and over) or pushing us forwards into the future (to pre-live them, often fretfully). As a consequence, we can end up caught in a maelstrom of conflicting thoughts and feelings, and it goes without saying that this has serious consequences for our 'quality' of life.

In particular, this has three profound effects:

we can miss out on being *here*, in the present
   moment;

we can live reactively at the constant demand of our
ego;
and we can judge our life continually, with narrow
and prematurely made-up minds.

Let's take each one briefly in turn.

(1) We miss out on being here, in the present moment

Just occasionally, we manage to be so wonderfully
absorbed in the present moment that all anxious thought
subsides, and we relax into the sheer good news of being
here, now.

Perhaps you can think of a time when this happened
to you: when you were swimming on a hot day in a pool
or river and it was truly enlivening; or you were playing
sport, and were 'in the zone'; or you were out for a walk
and turned a corner to catch a truly awe-inspiring sight.

Those times are rare, though wonderful. And I'm
sure our childhood memories are often so vivid because
we were better then at being in the present moment
without all that re-living or pre-living (in a sense, it's
only natural, as we had less to plan for or to worry
about). So if we close our eyes to summon a positive
childhood memory – try it now, if you like – it is usually
one that involves being *present*.

For me, it's playing cricket with my brother on a sunny
day in the school summer holidays; or sledging in the

woods on a dusky snow-filled late afternoon; or standing for what would seem like hours watching butterflies land on the purple blooms of buddleia in the back garden.

It might be building a den in the woods.

Or making sandcastles on a beach.

Or constructing a Lego palace.

*   *   *

If you are able to summon a similar memory of being present, why not pause for a moment, to give thanks for it, before you move on. Gratitude and appreciation are crucial ingredients when it comes to our own human flourishing.

*   *   *

The good news is that such vivid memories don't have to stay locked away gathering dust, because the present is – by its very definition – forever here, ready and willing to enfold us again within this eternal flow of 'now'. If we let it.

Perhaps we misunderstand nostalgia. It's not just that we yearn for the good old days: something deep within our soul reminds us that the beauty of the present, which we enjoyed so vividly as children, *is* still within reach.

(2) We live reactively at the demand of our ego

When our mental chatter draws us away from the present moment, we can deprive ourselves of the chance to live intentionally. It's like an internal monologue, which might tell us that we're about to make a fool of ourselves in public, or that we don't have what it takes, or that we need to look busy (or else!); whatever it's saying, this voice can quickly and easily become our default setting, because it's so all pervasive; and we can get so used to it that we end up living much of our life at its behest, without ever fully realising it, reacting unconsciously to its fears and insecurities.

We call this the voice of our ego. And if you want to identify it, just stop to notice when thoughts stream into your head that seem to be controlling, competing, or jealously comparing you to others. Your ego loves to make constant comparisons, so that you are driven to compete for, and to defend, your place in life. Often, too, you will experience a physiological reaction to the mental chatter, as stress rises within you, or you tense up.

* * *

(Pause to notice, for a few moments, whether you have any physical stress or tension in your body. It's easy to go through much of the day with a furrowed brow or a clenched jaw without even realising it. If you locate some physical tension, spend a minute or two relaxing your body before you read on.)

* * *

The voice of our ego – which loves to replay the comments once made by those in authority over us, and to mix them in with our own insecurities – takes control and we can end up acting almost exclusively upon the information it supplies, instead of allowing our actions to be informed by, and to flow from, a deeper source within. Soul.

True, we may not be like those typically big, boastful personalities we associate with having 'ego'; we may not feel forever driven to buy the flashier car or the bigger house. Yet our lives, nevertheless, are often just as affected by the ego's subtly insecure messages, which can leave us feeling worried, jealous, in fear of missing out, useless, and the rest. The background noise is tiresome, too; it keeps us awake at night. So we might drink too much to quieten the chatter. Or keep talking, to drown it out. Or stay busy so that we don't have to stop to consider it.

For as long as we act from our ego, then our life will, to a lesser or greater extent, involve controlling, competing and comparing; and, if we're all doing it, the world can feel like an unsettling and dissatisfying and sometimes dangerous place in which to live.

All the while, the option remains: of moving beyond these self-imposed limitations, to cultivate a deeper awareness of who we really are and what we can truly *offer* the world around us.

(3) We judge our life continually, with narrow and prematurely made-up minds

Here is the great loss: that if our lives are predominantly informed by the restless chatter of our insecure minds and the feelings they provoke, then we can cease to see the world around us, or our role within it, with any sense of child-like wonder or curiosity. We can narrow the possibilities or potential of our life, pre-judging situations and second-guessing what others are thinking (especially about us).

The upshot is that we live reactively, by pushing things away or pulling them tightly towards us, according to what we believe about any given situation.

When I pick my children up from school, my natural inclination is to ask them, 'How was your day?' To which one usually replies, 'Wonderful!' and the other, 'Awful.' But in even asking them this question, I am already teaching them to judge what they experience according to whether they like it or not. A life- or business-coach, who is trained to ask incisive, open questions, might perhaps alternatively wonder: 'What happened today? What did you learn? What did you notice? How did you grow?'

When we define each moment according to whether it's good or bad, and whether we like it or not, it becomes harder to see life, and our place within it, with eyes wide open. With our unconscious thought patterns – what we repeatedly tell ourselves about the world and other people and about what's coming next – we can thus diminish our sense of who we are and what we can bring of ourselves to the world, and we can end up facing much of life in the brace position, as if the plane is about to crash, instead.

Waking up

So it matters that we wake up to this, and try to stay more fully awake! Not just physically, at the start of each day, but to the gift of life that is ours to receive within every waking moment; and to the gift of being present, which we probably thought we'd left behind in childhood.

The positive alternative to mindlessness, then, is to become mindful. And the *practice* of mindfulness, which we'll consider now, is important, as it helps us to break up the mental chatter, and those patterns of insecure, judgemental thinking, so that we can give another voice – the voice of soul – the chance to speak. Mindfulness is, in fact, one of the most helpful ways of awakening, and staying awake, at our disposal, and one of the most effective ways to cope with, and to begin to counter, the world of ego that we are born into.

I said that the strength of mindfulness lies in its simplicity, clarity and effectiveness. Jon Kabat-Zinn, the man who is credited with developing mindfulness practice in an accessible and credible way for the Western world (and who founded the world-famous mindfulness-based stress reduction programme), defines it like this:

Mindfulness means
paying attention in a particular way;
on purpose,

in the present moment,
and non-judgmentally.

Which is elegantly simple.

Elsewhere, he describes it as 'wakefulness and open-hearted presence'.

If you could live your own life more fully awake, with open-hearted presence, think what difference it could make to the world around you.

Try this

At the close of this chapter, why not try to do something really simple, such as making and drinking a cup of tea or coffee, in a mindful way. That is, paying attention to the process – 'on purpose, in the present moment, non-judgmentally'.

One handy tip is to slow the process down a little, so that you are not rushing through it automatically. As the kettle boils, you might try taking a few slower, deeper breaths. Don't rush off to do something else meanwhile. Take the chance to pause. When you are ready to drink it, notice its warmth, its taste. Try not to think about everything else you have to do. (It will all be there for you when you get back to it.) And savour this moment, because it is precious.

19

2

How mindful practice can prepare us for the soulful life

You may just have enjoyed one of the best cups of tea you've had for a long time.

And you may also be experiencing a small but significant sense of restoration, simply through taking your time, and pausing to taste your drink, and, in a way, taste your life again. The good thing is, this doesn't cost very much either. (Although we do need to be brave enough to stop properly in the first place, which always costs us *something*.)

There are many creative ways to practise being 'wakeful with open-hearted presence', and we'll consider a few simple and effective ones to try now. The bedrock is meditation, a word that may evoke unhelpful connotations for you; but meditation needn't be all 'joss-sticks and whale-music', as a friend of mine recently and rather sceptically described it. Instead, it's something that any of us can practise in a common-sense way.

Professor Mark Williams, Emeritus Professor of Clinical Psychology at Oxford University, and one of the most helpful proponents of mindfulness, describes it as this: 'Calmly abiding in the present moment.' Which is a very good way of putting it indeed. *Calmly abiding in the present moment.* Once again, we don't have to make it much more complicated than that.

Calmly abiding

Of course, it's not always easy to abide calmly in the present moment, much as though we may like the sound of it. Our mind is quickly distracted, which is what puts most of us off sitting still in the first place. So there are techniques that can help us, and the most common is to use our breath as a focal point, or anchor.

So try this:

Sit peacefully, intentionally, for a few minutes. It helps to shut the door and to create a safe and quiet environment for yourself, free from distractions. Sit comfortably, with your back straight, and feet on the floor.

When you are ready, focus your attention on your breathing. Simply notice your breathing in, and your breathing out. You are not trying to achieve anything more than just noticing your breath. You are sitting still for the sake of it, aware of your breathing.

After a short while, you may notice that your mind has started to wander – and has led you off on a train of thought. That's OK. Use this as an opportunity to bring your attention gently back to your breathing, and to continue.

Do this each time you find you are 'lost in thought'. But don't worry, and don't feel frustrated with yourself; it's not a competition to sit for the longest time without mental chatter. Instead, aim to be *compassionate* with yourself each time you notice that your mind has wandered. In this way, compassion will grow within you, both towards yourself and others. And you will learn, as you go, to be less judgemental – especially because the person we are usually most judgemental with is our own self.

Instead, then, you'll become more objectively aware of where your mind tends to take you, and what it tends to focus on. And so, through meditation – through this process of *calmly abiding* – we can begin to notice both what and how we are thinking, and to identify the insecure voice of our ego, *and*, in time, to find a place of quiet assurance beyond it.

The benefits of meditation and mindful practice

'Numerous psychological studies', writes Professor Williams, 'have shown that regular meditators are happier and more content than average.' It's not just about feeling good, however; positive emotions are linked to a longer and healthier life, and so the medical ramifications that follow on naturally are measurable.

Anxiety, depression and irritability tend to decrease with meditation; memory can improve, reaction times speed up, relationships can strengthen, stress can decrease significantly, the immune system benefits, and meditation can even be effective in reducing the impact of conditions such as chronic pain and cancer, Williams suggests – as well as helping to relieve drug and alcohol dependency.

Of course, you don't have to wait until you are clinically ill to practise mindful meditation – the point is to check in with yourself little and often, especially to break up the compulsive patterns of thinking that can unhelpfully determine our reactions and diminish us in the process. Mindful practice helps us to stand back from our thoughts and feelings: to gain perspective in the midst of the action.

On training courses, I have led all sorts of different people (including roomfuls of sceptical senior managers) into periods of twenty minutes' silence, which is both a privilege and a challenge. While some remain bemused, most seem to appreciate the opportunity, for once, to sit in stillness without fiddling with a phone or being constantly interrupted. It can feel odd to start with, especially if you're sitting in silence with others; but push through that initial pain barrier and you soon find that you can settle into the process, to discover a different quality of space opening up around you: a space that was there all along if you had but paused to notice it. I've had people I've trained telling me that they still, some years on, make sure they 'press pause' regularly, to draw deeply again from that well of stillness.

* * *

A word of warning on how we view the benefits, however, before we continue. It is easy to fixate so much on what mindfulness can do for *me* that it ends up reducing the process to a mere self-help quick-fix – or even, dare I say, to a tool we can use for our exclusive advantage when we need it most. In the worst case, we can co-opt mindfulness to serve our ego; to manage our stress levels, for example, as we continue to clamber ever higher over others on the way to the top.

But that is to miss the point entirely. Mindfulness is not a tool to help us to conquer the world without getting too stressed. Instead, it quietens the anxious mind – and in those brief moments of respite, we remember something more of who we were, and who we are, and who we can be. This truly matters.

We remember that we are not our ego ... and that there is more, far more, to us than the mindless, automatic and unconscious patterns of compulsive thinking that so often drive our behaviour and fool us into living small. The mindful principles we have just considered, and the practices we will explore in the following pages (which are not exclusively the domain of mindfulness, but are shared by contemplatives the world over), take us to a profound and beautiful threshold, I believe, where, with quietened minds, we are better able, finally, to hear the gentle but compelling whisper of the soul.

3

Consciousness discipline – and the way the brain takes us deeper

Some practitioners refer to meditation as 'consciousness discipline' – not just because the word 'meditation' can put some people off, but also because it helps to explain something more fully about what's going on with the brain during the process.

Meditation can take us into deeper consciousness, which in turn can help us to reconnect with what's within us – our unique, inner aliveness – as well as what's without: especially that mysterious sense of aliveness or 'presence' that comes from life itself, through nature and culture, through other people, and from God; a presence that we're often oblivious to, but that is there to experience, nonetheless, and that we connect with more effectively when we are at a deeper level of consciousness.

It's hard, of course, to describe presence, but it's as though someone else is close by, even if you can't see them. You sense the presence, you tune in to it, and while you can't see it, it feels real enough, all the same. I've come to believe that it's there all the time, even when it doesn't feel like it; instead, it's *me* that isn't present to it, when I'm busy or distracted. (I love the way that the phrase 'God is nowhere' becomes, with the gentle tap of a space bar, 'God is now here'. It is when I take the time to pause and to open up a little gap that I sense God's presence most clearly.)

* * *

Developments in neuroscience are now providing us with a better understanding, almost daily it seems, of how practices such as meditation and stillness can help us not just to cope better, but to access more of our innate capacity, intelligence and potential. (They can also help us to understand why spiritual practitioners – such as monks, for example – have for millennia woven regular times of meditation and stillness into rhythms of work and communal activity.)

It may sound 'heavy' to speak of attaining deeper levels of consciousness, but we actually experience these all the time; the trick with meditation or 'consciousness discipline' is simply to find those deeper levels more intentionally, and so to bring extra facets of our being, such as deeper wisdom, creativity, empathy and intuition, to the surface more effectively.

Broadly speaking, we operate at four levels of consciousness, and for each level, there is a particular brain-wave that is most active: beta, alpha, theta or delta. (Brain-waves are created by synchronised electrical pulses from masses of neurons communicating with each other, and are detected by electroencephalogram or EEG machines, which measure the brain's electrical activity from just above the scalp.)

Our wakeful and day-to-day level of consciousness is where the beta brain-wave predominates. We need beta brain-waves to help us get the business of the day achieved: the task-focused, problem-solving stuff of life, which requires us to stay alert and focused. Without betas, we'd struggle to achieve anything!

However, when we begin to feel as if we have too much to do – we talk of spinning plates, when we've multiple tasks that are all competing for our undivided attention at once – then our stress levels begin to rise, and the body releases hormones such as adrenaline and cortisol in response to the beta waves going into overdrive. The increasing stress can be accompanied by a nasty sense of panic. I'm sure it's not just me who experiences this.

Below this surface level of consciousness is the more relaxing alpha zone, where the alpha brain-waves are most active. You find yourself here when you are dropping off to sleep, or when you are happily staring out to sea, or tinkering in the shed, or building Lego, or baking, or gardening – as well as when you're spending time in meditation. You may feel a bit day-dreamy when the alphas are doing their work – and perhaps you're the sort of person who gets so wrapped up in the narrative flow of a movie, for instance, that if someone sits on the sofa next to you and asks if you'd like a cup of tea, you don't even notice they're there. This is why intricate colouring books for adults are proving so popular today: they help people to get absorbed in a single enjoyable task, with relaxed concentration, without having to think too hard. A pleasant by-product of the brain's alpha-wave activity is that it helps one to feel happy, too, which is why these times can feel so enjoyable.

The alpha zone is highly significant not only because it offers much-needed, deeper rest from the 'busy' beta waves – preventing the build-up of stress, if we can find our way into it regularly enough – but also because it provides a threshold to the subconscious and unconscious activity of our brain. Without the alpha brainwaves we cannot become *consciously* aware of what's happening deeper down in our subconscious and unconscious – yet it's down there that some of our most significant work is done. In particular, the theta waves that predominate with the brain's subconscious activity are associated with times of peak creativity, as well as with empathy and intuition. The alphas help you to 'surface' all this good stuff.

Think about where and when you have your best ideas – those lovely, breakthrough moments of clarity or creativity that take your work or your thinking to the next level. It tends not to be when we are sitting at our computer or deliberately trying to grind out the work. Instead, it's more often when we're not thinking too hard – when we're in the shower or bath, for example, or out for a run or swim, or having a walk in the country, or waking up, or going to sleep. Without realising it necessarily, we've allowed the beta brain-waves to have a rest and the alphas to take the lead. These days, if I get really stuck, when I'm trying to write creatively, for example, I will go out for a run – not to think harder about my work, but to *stop* thinking about it. It takes some time for my mind to calm down, but once I have focused instead on my breathing, and have had a chance to breathe some air and work my body, then more often than not I will 'receive' an idea from seemingly out of the blue, from my subconscious. The alphas waves have helped this idea to the surface.

That's why we often say we'll 'sleep on it', for instance, if we're faced with a problem to solve, or a dilemma to grapple with. It gives our subconscious mind an opportunity to process what our conscious mind has struggled to resolve.

Paul McCartney awoke one morning with a tune in his head. In those first moments of awakening, it was so clear to him that, after hurrying to a piano to work out the music so that he didn't forget it, he called his friends in the music world to check if they knew who had written it – so convinced was he that he must have heard it somewhere else and copied it. Yet no one *had* heard the tune; it was original, and had formed in his subconscious without him having to force anything. In a sense, he only had to receive it as a gift and do something with it. And what he did was to write the song 'Yesterday'.

Isn't life, like that song, a great gift? But we have to receive it, actively!

Of course, that's not to say that hard work doesn't pay off, too; often, the brilliant idea that comes from left-field then requires hours, or days, or weeks, or sometimes even years of honing and crafting. Paul McCartney is known to be a fastidious and hugely dedicated musician, after all, and as the journalist Malcolm Gladwell has noted in his book *Outliers*, there is no substitute for relentless practice – in fact, 'researchers have settled on what they believe is the magic number for true expertise: ten thousand hours'. Yet the *inspiration* itself often seems to arrive when we least expect it.

All of which helps me to understand why I find myself more productively and effortlessly 'in flow' when I manage to incorporate regular, intentional 'time out' into the rhythms of my working schedule. It puts me back within the alpha zone and in better reach of the kind of material I couldn't necessarily 'think up' for myself. With a spiritual background, I've been used to spending times of stillness in meditation or prayer, and experiencing deeper levels of consciousness and connection; but these four levels of consciousness help me to understand more fully why (for example) one of my favourite lines from a psalm (46) in the Bible says, 'Be still!' And why it pays to become more intentional about doing this.

How could you personally enter the alpha zone, that place in which you are pleasantly absorbed in one thing, and where your mind is at rest? One friend told me that he experiences a sense of connection, calmness and (often) creative breakthrough when he goes out cycling. Perhaps you like to listen to a piece of relaxing music, or visit an art gallery, or sit on a bench and watch the world go by.

We all have those moments of breakthrough or connection that arrive seemingly 'out of the blue', as if by magic. But we can also be proactive about giving our alpha brain-waves the chance to help us, whether that's during the course of a day, a week, a month or a year. You can't go on holiday every day, but you can make a conscious choice to take a short walk in the fresh air, for instance. You may not feel you have time for a personal retreat every week, but you could put one in the diary once a quarter, and aim to spend a few hours at a place you find relaxing or inspiring.

Our busy culture affords little time for true stillness, and we often struggle to give ourselves or those around us the permission to pause for a deeper breath. It is a courageous person, then, who leaves their desk at work to have a lunch break, for instance, or walks to another floor to speak to a colleague instead of just e-mailing them – let alone who takes some time out to practise meditation or 'consciousness discipline'.

My friend Sophie, who runs a hospital Accident and Emergency department, was sceptical about the idea of meditation, but when, through a workshop, she experienced a few minutes of sitting quietly, she remembered just how good it was for her to pause, and how rarely she allowed herself to do it, and how important it was to remember to try. You don't have to have a high-octane job like hers to benefit, either: simply spending a few extra moments intentionally pausing between busy parts of the day – without checking emails, or anything else for that matter – can reconnect and re-energise you significantly.

It's a visionary leader (and we can all lead the way here) who is capable of finding deliberate ways to press pause (a few more practical examples will follow shortly) – to gain true and deeper rest from the stress of the busy beta waves, and to open up greater access to a world of intelligence that lies beyond the rational surface of thought, courtesy of that intriguing alpha threshold.

Wisdom from beyond the conscious mind

It takes great courage to step onto that threshold, especially when very few others are pausing for breath – but we find, when we do, a richer, more creative, intuitive, unorthodox, colourful and unexpectedly beautiful source of inspiration flowing from beyond the surface level of the conscious mind; for the deepening of our consciousness puts us in greater touch, I believe, with *soul* in a way that we would otherwise struggle to experience, and it connects us to a wisdom that is beyond the range of our own rational thought alone.

Who knows, precisely, where consciousness 'ends' and the wisdom of the soul begins? The Franciscan priest and author Richard Rohr, a great source of wisdom himself, states: 'Consciousness is as hard to describe as soul is hard to describe . . . perhaps because they are parts of the same thing.'

What matters is that we allow ourselves regular opportunity to go beyond the limits of the purely rational mind, to benefit from the riches of our deeper consciousness, and to connect with a wisdom that flows from down inside.

As the book of Proverbs in the Bible states, 'A wise person draws from the well within.' Draw deep!

4

Turning 'time out' into 'time in'

We can work towards deeper levels of consciousness (and awareness) both through taking 'time out', when we ring-fence some space for ourselves in a structured way, and through becoming more present and aware within the action of the day as it unfolds – which I call 'time in'.

Time out could last for as long as a week away, if you need to contemplate something as major as a career change or house move, for instance, or it could be as short as a few minutes' 'breather' between household chores. But it's about discipline. You won't run a marathon if you don't train in a self-disciplined way, gradually building up the exercise; and likewise, you won't reap benefits from practices such as stillness and meditation if you don't engage with them regularly. You might start with a few minutes per day of simple meditation, or even just turning off your phone and being present to what's before you – which you can then extend as time goes on, or repeat at regular times throughout the day (such as an afternoon break, or the journey home from work, or your walk to the school gates).

You could also begin to take a few moments to pause, for instance, as you are about to make a difficult phone call, or as you're about to lead a meeting or make a presentation. Any 'time out' like this can positively disrupt our unconscious patterns of thinking, and quieten our worried thoughts (which usually grow louder before a presentation or a difficult phone call!) – and thus help you to bring your attention back to the present moment, on purpose, without judgement.

It can help you awaken to *this* moment with open-hearted presence – which will benefit not just you but those you're about to meet or speak with or lead. Don't judge them ahead of time: be open to the possibilities!

However, the important thing to remember – and this, in a sense, is the great challenge – is to *stay* aware and awake between those specific moments of 'time out'. It's the 'time in' that provides us with the opportunity to be present at precisely those moments when we are most likely to get stuck on autopilot, or react automatically from ego.

Any part of your day can be converted into an opportunity to try 'time in' with open-hearted presence.

You could start by identifying those periods in the day when you're most likely to switch to autopilot. Simply by doing this, you'll become more aware and better prepared to redeem those times, and to use them, instead, to enrich the rhythm of your day. It could be your commute, when you put the car radio on automatically (or stick your headphones in on the train or bus). It could be your regular trip to the shops, or to school. Journeys are especially helpful to focus on, as we tend to wish them away; the age-old question asked by children – 'Are we nearly there yet?' – never truly leaves our system! Yet rather than wishing you were there already, which usually induces stress, try calmly abiding in the present moment for the duration. Another friend of mine, when she cycles to work, very specifically uses the time she spends waiting at traffic lights to be mindful. This helps her to remember that the journey in to work is as much of a blessing as the rest of the day, and that life isn't about always having to get somewhere, but about being *here*, in this present moment, and pausing to enjoy it. Similarly, you might use the times when you are waiting in a supermarket queue, or at the bank, or waiting for a train to arrive – times when you could often feel frustrated – to enjoy the fact that you are simply here, and alive, and present.

Awake at the wheel

Have you ever reached your destination only to realise you've been so lost in thought that you have no idea how you got there safely? It's scary! But it's also a powerful metaphor for the way we live; chunks of time go missing when we are lost in thought or distracted, and it's as though we're asleep at the wheel. So any form of journey can be an excellent exercise in staying wakeful.

Whatever your mode of transport, before you set off, you could spend a few moments pausing. We're often in such a hurry that we rush off, without composure. By pausing before you go, you can become more intentional about the way you travel. If you're cycling, just wait a moment. Feel the grip on the handlebars. Look up, look around you. If you're driving, take five seconds before turning the ignition. If you're walking, stop, and breathe, and move off with poise!

As you go, try to be aware of three things: what you see, what you hear, and how you feel. This will keep you mindful of the journey itself. When your mind wanders, bring it back to these three things alone. And notice what you notice!

Travelling like this can help us to avoid that awful anxiety of being late (you can't get there quicker by driving or riding anxiously, and you will arrive in a much better state if you 'park' your stress along the way); it can ease your annoyance at fellow passengers or road users, as you simply notice any thoughts that flood into your head when someone cuts you up or angers you by playing their music too loudly (and by noticing them, you will avoid reacting instantly, thus reducing the risk of conflict or road rage); and if you're on a boring journey, staying present can help you not to get lost in swathes of unhelpful internal chatter as you go. Mental energy is, in fact, a depletable resource, according to the leadership and energy expert Tony Schwartz, and even those conversations we have in our head when we re-live or pre-live arguments or disputes can use up energy we might otherwise have saved for arriving fresh and ready to go.

Imagine arriving at your destination – work, back home, at a friend's house, or at a meeting – fully present, calm, and ready.

* * *

If this feels too much, you could designate a regular day (or morning) each week to try to practise 'time in'. Or you might like to set your alarm for regular periods throughout the day, as a 'wake-up' call and a reminder not to sleep-walk your way through the day.

The point is not to achieve a perfect day – which is forever out of reach! – but to break up the perpetual state of busyness-as-usual, and to keep waking from our slumbers, and ... to find ourselves on that threshold where the soul may stir once more. Exercises like this need not be just about damage limitation alone

– calming down, de-stressing, coping – but they can also prepare us to live with soul.

Count ten breaths

One regular way I have found to guide me back into the present moment, with conviction and compassion – especially when I'm about to get upset or lose my temper – is to count ten breaths.

This is a simple but incredibly effective way to pause, within the heat of the moment, and to make sure you don't react from your ego. As soon as you know you are losing your cool (and if you have the opportunity to walk away for a few moments, do) start to deepen your breathing, and to bring your awareness and attention to your breath. You can then count ten breaths in and out, if you like, or simply stay focused on your breathing for about a minute.

You will find that in this time, your heart rate will have lowered, you will have created distance between yourself and the activating event, you will have noticed how tempted you were to react automatically, and in what manner . . . and you will thus be far better placed to respond in a measured, compassionate and fruitful way.

* * *

If you'd like to be a little more intentional still, the Buddhist monk Thích Nhất Hạnh advocates combining a focus on breathing with walking, through five simple steps:

Step **one** is to become aware of your in-breath, and your out-breath, and call them your in-breath and out-breath.

Step **two** is to follow your in-breath from its start to its end, then follow your out-breath from *its* start to end, and keep that going.

Step **three** is to become aware of your body as you breathe. Notice your breath entering and leaving your body, and the effect it has.

Step **four** is to release the tension in your body.

And step **five** is to incorporate those first four steps while you take a walk. So find somewhere to try this – it could be your garden, or somewhere private at first; but you can always develop awareness on the go, even along your local high street, walking to the bus stop or on your way to meet a friend. Each step can become truly enjoyable, if you let it. (I also try this when I am out for a training run, which is helpful because it's easy to wish that the exercise is over before it has begun!)

You are not trying to get anywhere in particular with a walk or a run like this, so it's a different type of movement from the start. You may find it helpful to slow down your walking as you go. But what Thích Nhất

Hạnh observes is inspiring. 'The real miracle is not to fly or walk on fire. The real miracle is to walk on the Earth, and you can perform that miracle at any time,' he writes.

The miracle is to be present. And I've found that these five short steps can help you, in a gradual but intentional way, to 'show up' more fully here and now. To walk through life remembering that it's all a miracle.

I'm aware that not everyone can walk, of course. But an exercise like this can be modified, or recontextualised. Once when I was leading a retreat for a group of people out in the countryside, I had the privilege of accompanying a wonderful lady in a wheelchair who had suffered from a debilitating illness and lost the use of her legs. During the retreat, I invited the group to do a short 'walk of awareness', in which we went through the five steps above, and finished by having a gentle, slow walk through a meadow. I was, needless to say, anxious about how my new friend in the wheelchair would react to being asked to perform the miracle of walking on Earth, when she couldn't. But she responded enthusiastically and magnificently, savouring every moment as she wheeled herself slowly through the meadow, and became mindfully present in a slightly different way. She found it an inspiring part of the day.

Journalling

It's also very useful to write things down. The physical act of (hand)writing a journal actually enables your brain to process things in a different way, as you reflect back on your day or week; specifically, it can help your brain to re-live an experience. Handwriting also gets you away from a screen of course, which is usually a positive thing.

I have found personally that when I write, I allow thoughts to arise – along with insights and perceptions – that I didn't know were there until I began the writing. It's a creative way of processing the day you've had. You can write down what you've noticed (that you might otherwise have forgotten about all too soon), or how you've been feeling, or what has particularly inspired or challenged you. You could reflect upon what you have found difficult or have been struggling with, or how you have noticed yourself reacting, or what ideas have been bubbling up inside you . . .

The process of writing can help you to enter the alpha zone, where ideas can emerge *through* the writing, instead of you having to think them up in advance before putting them down on paper. I have discovered ideas of 'my own' through this way of writing that I didn't even realise I 'knew' until I put pen to paper.

This, of course, is true for all artistic endeavours. It's through the process itself that you are better able to lose yourself in the activity and thus to find something beneficial within, flowing through you. So keep the channel open! If you like painting or drawing, you can't carry an easel around with you all day, but you can find moments with a small sketch book or notepad. Imagine if, every time you were tempted to glance at your phone, check texts, surf the Internet or look at social media, instead you drew, sketched, doodled, mind-mapped or wrote. What a creative pathway this could open up for you!

You don't need to be a writer to journal, and no one else needs to see your work, by the way; in fact, it helps if you decide in advance that your reflections will be for no other eyes but your own. In this way you are more likely to explore honestly and openly, instead of 'editing' as you go for the benefit of a hypothetical 'someone else'.

You might like to buy a notebook or journal that will inspire you to get started and to keep going; one that is perhaps a little more special or expensive, and that you will positively enjoy returning to. Find one that feels soulful! And try to decide what time of day would work best for you to do some writing. You don't need to carve out huge swathes of your schedule. It could be little and often, once a day, or even once a week.

The idea is not to create an extra burdensome task, but to release your creativity through an enjoyable process. Think of it as facilitating the creative flow within you, so that you can process, and record, and surface what you've noticed about both your day and your life – as well as giving expression to what might otherwise pass *unnoticed* within your subconscious. Using a journal to be mindful in this way can become a very soulful experience – and one that takes us closer to the point where a calm mind can open the way for the soul to speak . . .

One retired gentleman told me recently of how, thirty years ago, he had watched a TV programme about a severely disabled set of twins. He had been so touched by the programme, he said, that he did something unusual (for him): he wrote about the programme, and his resultant feelings, in a notebook, which he kept (and in which he continued to make occasional entries). Three decades later, the man's son had a child who was born with the same condition as the twins from the TV programme. When this little girl died, aged three, the process of writing a second journal entry, beneath the one about the twins, helped a grieving grandfather, he said, to express and explore his feelings at the unspeakably sad loss his family had suffered.

Do something for the sake of doing it – not for the sake of getting it done!

There's a crucial difference here that is subtle yet significant.

When we end up trying to get through every task we face in the day merely for the sake of getting it done, then we can get through hours, days, weeks and sometimes months just . . . getting through. While we are still trying to finish *this* thing, our focus is on the *next* thing. All of which means that we are rarely present.

How much of our life is spent trying to get this one thing done in order to move on to the next? I dread to think.

The washing-up is a good example – or unloading the dishwasher, if you are fully automated! If you're rushing through it for the sake of getting on, you will be wishing away a small but regular chunk of your daily routine that could otherwise be an opportunity to remember that you are *here*. Try to focus on the dishes, and notice small details you might otherwise not have noticed; be aware of what you are thinking and feeling, and *breathe*. When your mind starts to strain forwards, wishing you'd already finished, pause for a moment, smile, relax . . . You might reflect on the nature of water itself, and be grateful that it's plumbed into your house, and has the power to cleanse, and to refresh, and to sustain. Try to bring all your attention to the way the water feels against your skin, and enjoy it. Listen to the sound it makes. As you handle your crockery, you might like to be mindful of those who usually eat or drink from it, and to hold them in your loving attention, or to pray quietly that they find true and satisfying nourishment in their life.

By attending to what's at hand, and doing it for the sake of doing it, you can liberate yourself to savour what you'd otherwise describe as a chore – instead of wishing yet another small part of your precious and unrepeatable life away.

The point is not to get out of it, but to get *in* to it.

And then do one thing at a time

This is the natural step on from doing something for the sake of doing it. And it's an excellent way to stay in the zone. When we 'multi-task', we try to do several things at once without ever giving any of them the full and undivided quality of attention they require and deserve. (After all, how did you feel when a friend was trying to have a conversation with you while checking their phone all the time?) The result is that we bring sub-optimal energy and attention to everything, and our life becomes a pale imitation of what it could really be like; an endless round of 'task switching', which is usually unsatisfying and unproductive.

You can only truly do one thing at a time, unless you're doing something as automatic as walking (and even then, as we've seen with breathing, we need to bring our full attention to it if we are to remember to do it well!). So try doing just one thing, followed by another, for a limited period of time like a morning, and see how you get on. You may well be surprised at the speed with which you get things done, let alone the quality with which you do them, for a change.

One thing, and then the next, with grace, poise, care and love. What a difference that can make. Especially if you're the kind of friend who usually checks their phone when they're also trying to listen to someone face to face.

*   *   *

Imagine the difference it could make to you if all the people you worked with, or lived with, or you found yourself sharing a train carriage with today, were awake with open-hearted presence! Wouldn't that be inspiring and contagious? Especially in the context of today's Western culture in which, perplexingly, despite having so much, most of us seem to have such little peace, calmness, assurance, time.

Sadly, the chances are that the next person you encounter will *not* be quite as present, compassionate and engaged as you might like. However, if *you* are, you can make a potentially immeasurable difference to them and to the quality of their day, and that's quite a start, and a wonderful place from which, now, to continue.

Interlude: Are you ready for adventure?

Let's stop and think for a moment. The point is not to use techniques such as mindfulness simply to help us to become 'better adapted cogs' in the otherwise toxic machinery of contemporary life, as the depth psychologist Bill Plotkin once put it. If we're trying to be better adapted cogs, then all we're doing ultimately is helping the toxic machinery to run more smoothly. It's like the management team of the chemical weapons factory employing mindfulness techniques to help them cope better with the pressures of killing people more effectively.

Neither should we see mindfulness as a way of striving to reach some kind of imagined state of spiritual perfection. It doesn't exist (at least, not in the way most of us think it might) and the sad consequence of becoming spiritual for the sake of it, or because it seems like a cool lifestyle choice, is usually that we lose touch with our flesh-and-blood humanity in the process. We become like cardboard cut-outs of ourselves. Please note: the true goal of spirituality is not to become more spiritual, but to become more fully human.

Have you ever met someone who – instead of making you feel bad about yourself because they're so 'good', so sorted, so together – seems to bring you to life, and inspires you to greater heights and depths? They lift you, almost without doing anything at all. They inspire you, just by the way they are. They help you, somehow, mysteriously, to feel connected, alive again, humane, accepted, loved . . . just through the way that they look at you, or through the way they greet you, or through the way they listen to you with undivided attention.

It doesn't happen all that often, it's sad to say. But they *are* out there, such people, if you keep your eyes open for them.

I remember the time I interviewed the celebrated author, philosopher and poet-priest John O'Donohue for a newspaper. He bustled in late for our breakfast meeting at the hotel where he was staying during his appearance at an arts festival called Greenbelt. I'd been waiting for him for quite some time, in increasing frustration – yet as soon as he found me, the frustration lifted; you could sense in a moment that this was a man who overflowed with something *more* . . . he was engaging, mischievous, human in the best kind of way. We usually speak of people having 'hidden depths', but his depths were not hidden at all. We sometimes call this gravitas, or presence.

He apologised with a grin for keeping me waiting, explaining, as he sat down, that he and a friend had got carried away the previous night with some good conversation and some even better single-malt whisky. 'But don't worry,' he whispered conspiratorially, and with a wonderful Irish lilt, as he leaned in: '*The bottle didn't die without spiritual necessity!*'

I had been expecting to meet someone more ... well, *serene*; Zen-like, perhaps, and a little out of reach – which, come to think of it, is how the 'successful' spiritual life so often seems to most of us. Yet here he was, somehow far more real than that. Well *within* reach. And that spoke to me, more than anything, because he also put me within reach of myself once more. Of my own depths and heights. As the wonderful Quaker writer and educationist Parker Palmer once put it, 'We sense that something is missing in our lives and search the world for it, not understanding that what is missing is us.'

*   *   *

I believe the soulful life is fully within reach, if we did but know it. Some of us can try so hard to be 'good' at spirituality – to be forever reaching for the unreachable state, if you like – that we can end up missing the point of life in its fullness. In the meantime, a few rare souls manage to flood the space around them with a life and a presence that is so real, vivid, energetic and compassionate that they inspire us to believe we can do likewise.

They have soul.

And we know it.

Because deeper down, below the layers, the masks, the personas, the mental chatter, the defences, the striving . . . we have soul, too.

As John O'Donohue and I chatted, I asked him why it's so hard, in today's culture, to live meaningful, authentic lives – and his thoughts turned quickly to soul. This is what that Irishman with the hangover told me, without even having to stop to think about it: 'Soul is a dangerous thing to have,' he said. 'It links you into the infinite, whether you like it or not, and won't let you rest happy in your mediocrity or escapism.'

* * *

And that's perhaps why so many of us do pull back into the comfort zone of ego. There *is* rest in mediocrity and escapism, albeit an unsatisfying kind of rest, and we can grow to like it. Likewise, we can fear the danger that comes with awakening further. When the Pevensie children walk through the wardrobe and into their Narnian adventures, they don't know where they will end up. When Neo has to decide in the *Matrix* whether to take the blue pill or the red pill, he knows that if he chooses to take the red pill, life will never be the same again; he will awaken to a clearer and deeper form of reality than the world of distraction and entertainment within the Matrix. How often we passively accept lives of mediocrity and escapism.

Do you *want* to be well?

Jesus had a way of asking powerful questions, one of which is particularly relevant for us here. Once, he met a man who had been ill for thirty-eight years, who was waiting beside a pool that was believed to have healing qualities. Jesus turned to the man and asked: 'Do you want to get well?'

It sounds almost outrageously rude. But I wonder how many of us really do want to be well, if it means making courageous lifestyle changes, or deciding to live on a lower salary (for the sake of higher-quality time, for instance), or changing the way we shop, or some such. You'd think we'd love to get away from the tread-mill of busyness-as-usual, and certainly from our more harmful patterns of living and being, as fast as we could, given the chance. Yet so often we struggle to imagine how life could be much different; it's partly because we're afraid to stop, for fear of feeling guilty or lazy; and it's often because we find a sense of identity through busyness or even burnout. When so many of us wear busyness as a badge of honour, it takes courage to choose a different path.

Do we want to be well?

Do we want to flourish?

These are not rhetorical questions. We have to face and answer them if we are to move on, whether individually, or as families, or teams at work, or wherever we find ourselves. If we are to build on the gains of mindfulness, and press in to a different way of being, instead of simply using a few techniques to help us to cope better with the stressful lives we've created for each other, then this must spring from a desire to be transformed ourselves, and to help transform the world around us for the sake of others.

Be transformed . . .

You don't have to be engaged deliberately in mindful practice or contemplative spirituality in order to experience true moments of awakening, of course. A sudden bereavement usually serves as a powerful (if undesired) wake-up call, and likewise the diagnosis of a serious illness or the shock news of redundancy can shake us out of our mediocrity and escapism; just as the unexpected sight of a kingfisher darting along a river can cause the soul to stir, or cradling a newborn baby, or hearing a song for the first time in years that meant so much to you.

All of which, in turn, opens up an intriguing, unfamiliar space, deeper within us and even *around* us. A soul space.

We have started our explorations 'up there' in the mind, because it's crucial to wake up, perhaps for the first time, to how the voice of the ego, which makes its presence felt through the anxious mind, can be so influential. If we can recognise the ego for what it is, however, and if we are able to quieten that debilitating inner monologue, this is where it gets exciting: because transformation becomes possible. Things *can* change, if we want them to. And we can change, if we want to.

There is a deeply profound line, written by Paul, in the Bible, which says, 'Be transformed by the renewing of your mind.'

I used to think this meant, 'Believe the right things and you will go to heaven.' But that was, of course, a simplistic and distorted reading of the text! Paul wasn't talking about belief in terms of being in the right or the wrong club. Instead, if your mind is genuinely renewed – if the voice of the ego subsides enough to stop dominating your life – then your soul, that true and unique source of energy and identity within and around you, can finally make its presence felt.

You will start to be transformed into the person you truly are.

You knew something was missing from your life; it was *you*.

At first, when we quieten the mind, it might just feel like a void; a happy respite from the internal monologue. A rest from over-thinking. A pleasant lack of anything in particular. A chance to breathe. An opening. Blessed relief! All of which is to be truly savoured, in itself, just like the glorious absence of noise when the pneumatic drill outside your window finally stops. Or when the guns finally fall silent in a time of war.

Yet the good news – the great news, in fact – is that there is far more to this than mere absence: for there is also a *presence*. In those moments of peace, we are far better able to sense the soul. And it's almost impossible to put into words, but it's the same kind of feeling we might get from stepping off a busy street into the sanctuary of an ancient little church, or strolling around the corner of a cliff-top path to behold a breathtaking landscape – and as we do, we reconnect with something beautiful and profound within us.

The mystery, I believe, is that through these times of awakening, whether they're intentional or not, hairline cracks begin to form upon the hard and shiny surface of our ego, which begins to split, little by little, like the shell of an acorn ... And that's a tantalising place in which to find ourselves, because the cracks signal that something new may now start to stretch and grow from deeper within.

From a place beyond the mind.

Part 2
Reaching in for soul: awakening to our unique, inner aliveness

5

Awake, my soul!

Mindfulness, then, helps us to quieten the ego effectively enough that we find ourselves standing on the threshold of soul, but there we have a choice: retreat back into the comfort zone of the ego once more, or push out of the comfort zone and into the often unexplored territory of soul – to discover more of what our unique, inner aliveness really looks like when it finds expression.

For we do each have a uniqueness that matters. We have unique physical fingerprints, and we touch the world around us uniquely through our presence, too. We each have unique physical retinas, and no two people ever see life in exactly the same way.

There's a line in my favourite psalm in the Bible, Psalm 139, which says, 'I praise you because I am fearfully and wonderfully made.' It is easy, in the busyness of the day, to forget that there is something uniquely wonderful about every single person, including our own self. The Bible also suggests that we bear the 'image' of God – which suggests to me that we have a fearfulness and wonder to us that cannot, and will not, in the end, be confined to the roles we play and the labels we are given in life. We reflect something of God, and life itself, through who we are, in a way that no one else does. Let's not neglect that extraordinary privilege!

We are poised, then – if we so choose – to step 'further up, and further in' (as the Pevensie children are invited to do at the conclusion of C.S. Lewis's *Narnia Chronicles*). Something fearful and wonderful is within reach: the opportunity of discerning, and welcoming, the presence of our unique soul. It takes attention and awareness to recognise this presence, welcome and even befriend it, but with practice, we can tune in more skilfully and intentionally.

If we think, however, that we can summon soul as if it's a genie in a lamp who is there to grant our wishes for a better life, we must think again. This is an enigmatic process; the soul – this missing sense of 'me', if you like – will not yield easily to dissection. We cannot pin it down, like a butterfly in a collection, and that's a big challenge for our rational minds, which prefer to be in control and to have things categorised efficiently. If we could split our self into easily identifiable parts to see how we fit together, then we might solve the puzzle of our life. But we can't, and that's part of the joy of the creative process of discovering what soul is all about. We'll consider a few ways now of how some people have tried to 'capture' the idea of soul.

Twenty-one grams

At the turn of the twentieth century, the US physician Duncan MacDougall tried an experiment to measure the mass of the soul. He wanted to see whether it was possible to detect any loss in weight of a human body at the point of death. Through his limited experiments (with six people, most of whom were dying from tuber-culosis) he deduced that the body lost a consistent twenty-one grams (three-quarters of an ounce) at the very point of death, which, he believed, could be attrib-uted to the soul's departing.

Unsurprisingly, his work has been discredited since, because his findings were too inconsistent, his methods were too basic, and the sample study was too small. Nevertheless, at the time it seemed plausible enough to be reported in the *New York Times*, and it remains a vivid idea that has captured the cultural imagination powerfully enough to resurface in different artistic forms since, such as in the 2003 Hollywood film *21 Grams*.

The science may not be right, but nevertheless, the idea of the soul being 'substantial' is quietly compelling. Twenty-one grams, as the film's trailer says, is 'the weight of a stack of nickels, the weight of a chocolate bar, the weight of a hummingbird. It is also the weight of the human soul.' I love that gentle association – implied by the words and also the film's imagery – of the soul with a hummingbird. Both seem so light, so colourful, so furtive and mysterious . . .

Duncan MacDougall hoped in vain that an X-ray machine would one day be able to show us what the soul looks like. It remains camera shy to this day, an enigma; neuroscience helps us to understand consciousness, but though we sense the soul, we cannot prove its existence – which is why we need, more than ever, the artistry of poets, musicians, painters, writers, theologians, as well as psychologists and philosophers, to help us to explore and express what soul might look like, feel like, taste like, sound like, in our life. I think we all know we need it, even if we don't know exactly what it is we need.

To start with, perhaps, we simply need courage, to step onto the path that leads us *inside*, to explore our inner landscape, and to search our self for soul. And just because we cannot see it under a microscope, it doesn't mean it's not there. We simply have to find other ways to tune in to it instead.

Something that doth live

I'd like you to imagine, for a moment, that we continue beyond physical death . . . and then try to imagine who you are after you have died.

I don't think many of us would imagine ourselves to be the sum of the exterior parts of our life: the clothes we've just bought, or the aftershave or perfume, or the job title. You can't take any of those with you anyway, I am told. We're more likely, I believe, to summon a distillation of our soulful inner self . . .

And imagine that this 'you of you' – when it's not drowned out by the chatter of ego, or hidden by the masks you sometimes wear to protect your vulnerability – were heightened somehow. There's an application on my smart-phone that enhances my photographs. It fills out the colours of the picture, and sharpens the focus, and brings it to life. Imagine that the colours of your soul were intensified, and its edges brought into focus, so that you could see it more clearly, as if you were meeting your true self for the first time, instead of the pale imitation.

It's fascinating how often there is a deep, soulful radiance about a dying person, even while they are physically withering – as though their own true self is finally emerging from behind the layers. Wouldn't it be wonderful if we didn't have to wait until just before death for the 'you of you' and the 'me of me' to be revealed? It seems to me that this is part of the art of soulfulness: to live from the radiant sense of self that requires few of life's adornments and embellishments to weigh it down or disguise it.

We can look at it from the other end of our life's journey, too, as Wordsworth did in his poem 'Ode:

Intimations of Immortality from Recollections of Early Childhood', where he explores the idea that we *arrive* in this world with a far more glorious identity than we realise, and which we quickly begin to lose touch with. We arrive, he writes, 'trailing clouds of glory from God, / who is our home'. Our birth, he writes, is 'but a sleep and a forgetting'. We glimpse only 'shadowy recollections' of this greater identity; nevertheless, there is reason to be hopeful, even joyful:

> O joy! that in our embers
> Is something that doth live.

In our embers, the embers of all our projects, our work, our relationships, our hopes, our fears, our dreams . . . 'is something that doth live'. What a prospect: to discover what that unburnable something is, and to revive it.

* * *

Sometimes, it's about knowing where to look, and having the courage to search in places other than magazines, adverts or the mirror for clues as to our true and possibly missing identity. Perhaps we miss some of the clues that could imbue the story of our life with a richer sense of meaning altogether. It's possible. In this extract from Douglas Coupland's soulful book *Life After God*, his narrator reflects on where and how we might look differently for life:

I thought of how every day each of us experiences a few little moments that have just a bit more resonance than other moments ... we share a hotel elevator with a bride in her veils, say, or a stranger gives us a piece of bread to feed to the mallard ducks in the lagoon; a small child starts a conversation with us ...

If we were to collect those fleeting encounters and record them in a notebook over a few months, he suggests, we might see trends emerge – certain voices, perhaps, that have been trying to speak through us.

'We would realise', Coupland's narrator concludes, 'that we have been having another life altogether; one we didn't even know was going on inside us. And maybe this other life is more important than the one we think of as being real ... So just maybe it is these small silent moments which are the true story-making events of our lives.'

What a thought – that each of us experiences a few little moments that have 'just a bit more resonance'. You might not have bumped into many brides in the lift recently, but I wonder what has touched or resonated with you, which you may have forgotten about, or neglected; a line from a song, an unexpected postcard, a moment of serendipity with a stranger that rang strangely true. Moments of loving connection between you and the world around you, which create a different kind of story, of a different quality and nature, and a story that you can tune in to with increasing intentionality, if you are awake to it.

*　　*　　*

'All you can ever achieve is a sense of your soul,' writes John O'Donohue. 'You gain little glimpses of its light, colours and contours. You feel the inspiration of its possibilities and the wonder of its mysteries.'

We cannot dissect it, but instead must sense it, intuit it, wait for it, and notice when it whispers to us, or nudges from within, and connects us meaningfully with the world around us. We'll explore all sorts of ways of connecting more deeply with soul as we go, in order to live more of our days *with* soul as a result.

But I'd like to tip things upside down for a few moments. Because it's easy to slip back into ego as we become excited about the prospect of discovering soul.

It's all very well to talk of having soul, or having *a* soul . . . but as soon as we begin to speak in terms of ownership, we're in danger of veering off the soulful path, because we can begin thinking again in a possessive way, and from the perspective of the ego. Our soul is not like some trophy husband or wife who is there for our pleasure and benefit, to drape on our arm as some kind of adornment when we feel the need to show the world that we actually have one. A soul, that is.

'Never tell a child', said the celebrated Scottish author, poet and minister George Macdonald, 'you have a soul. Teach [them], you are a soul who has a body . . .'

You *are* the soul. And that's quite a leap for most of us to make, mentally, as well as emotionally and spiritually, because we tend to think of ourselves in terms of being the person, or even just the body, who *has* a soul, not the other way round.

Earthing the relationship between body and soul

Different traditions have varying understandings of 'soul', of course: Buddhists speak of the 'original nature', Hasidic Jews refer to the 'divine spark', Quakers call it the 'inner teacher' or 'inner light' . . . They all point to something similar: a sense of what I would call our unique, inner aliveness.

But the danger has always been, with all forms of spirituality, that we can end up with a false dichotomy between body (= bad) and soul (= good), which in turn emphasises our need to escape this awful world and its fleshly temptations, to take refuge in the realm of 'pure' spirit. But this is not my idea of soulfulness!

The Judaeo-Christian tradition, for me, counters this dichotomy, emphasising instead the dynamic interplay between body and soul *as a whole*. And this is what leads me, in fact, to my own definition of the soulful life, which describes this interplay in the context of

67

the loving relationships which the soul, ultimately, establishes.

Soulfulness, then:

gives flesh-and-blood expression
to our unique, inner aliveness,
through a loving reconnection with all parts of life.

I say 'gives', because I do believe that the embodied expression of our soulful self is a true gift to the world, and one that we should not hold back.

'The soul is the animation of the body, and the body is the incarnation of the soul,' as the biblical scholar J.K. Chamblin puts it. I add, in my definition above, that this interplay finds expression most profoundly through loving relationships with all parts of life, including, most significantly, with each other, with God and with creation. It is never isolated, even when we are alone, because our soul not only defines us uniquely, but also connects us, relentlessly and lovingly, to the soul of others.

This is crucial to keep in mind, for soulfulness is *not* about floating away on the spiritual clouds; quite the contrary. Soul might be almost impossible to describe and to see, yet it is not ethereal, nor is it isolated; *soul responds to touch*, and as such is not some flighty and out-of-reach spiritual state, but is as simple and beautiful as a hand that reaches out to be held.

Let me explain just a little more about what I draw from the Judaeo-Christian understanding of soul, specifically in terms of the body and the physical world, before we move on to ask, practically, how we can sense more of our unique, inner aliveness for ourselves.

*   *   *

The Hebrew word *nephesh* is the one that's most often translated as 'soul' from the Hebrew scriptures, but it has at least eight derivations: a living being, life, self, a person, desire, passion, appetite and emotion. And it's this breadth of meaning that leads people such as the Hebrew scholar Scott Morrin to describe *nephesh* as 'your whole being'.

In the Bible's account of creation in Genesis (which is not necessarily meant to be taken literally, but is written as a poem that contains profound theological reflection on where we came from, and who we are) we read that God formed a human body from the dust, and breathed life into it, whereupon the man 'became a living soul' (*nephesh*). Sometimes this is also translated as 'a living *being*'. The inference from this passage is not that God made a body and popped a soul inside it; instead, God brought the dust to life, and the dust became the being, a whole creature in itself.

In the New Testament, Paul (who was responsible for shaping so much *Christian* theology in its earliest days) finds himself influenced more by this Hebraic way of thinking than by the contemporary Greek tendency to elevate 'spirit' above 'flesh'. In Paul's writing, as

Chamblin puts it, 'The body is integral to God's good creation; and the soul is not a "higher self" ... Within creation the soul, far from being destined to overrule or escape the body, fulfils its purpose precisely in relation to the body.'

The *soul*ful life (denoted by the Greek word 'psyche'), then, is a bodily existence. Most biblical scholars, concludes Chamblin, see soul and body as 'indivisible (though conceptually distinguishable)'.

* * *

This is not to deny, in the writing of Paul and throughout Christian theology, the profound sense of inner struggle between what is so helpfully described by contemplative Christian writers, such as Father Richard Rohr, as the relationship between our 'false sense of the self' and our 'true self'.

The false sense of self is the anxious, insecure ego, which hijacks us through the mind. The 'fall', which is described in the biblical account of the creation of the world that we find in Genesis, helps us to see this false sense of the self from within the context of our relationship with God, which has been disconnected from its original flourishing state. A common misperception is that the Bible denounces us all as worthless sinners, but Genesis states very clearly that in the beginning, what God made was 'very good'. In a sense, when we manage to awaken to the anxious ego, and settle more deeply and assuredly back into the ways of the soul, we are able to enter and experience more of what we might call our 'original blessing'.

The recalibration we require most urgently, then, is between the *mind* and the soul, as we enter the path that leads us into soulfulness. Over time, and with practice, the mind, which has been commandeered by the ego for far too long, is gently released to start doing what it does best, which is to place its great powers of thinking in the service of the soul and of the soul's gracious leading.

So the tail no longer wags the dog.

Soul is not something to have, then, but to *be*. It has a life of its own. And when we remember this, we are able to step more fully into the soulful life.

We're going to move on now to consider the simple yet profound idea that when we look for the soul, we find ourselves looking *from* the soul. When we seek to tune in to the soul in any way – using any of our senses in particular – we actually begin to sense *through* the soul: we learn to look soulfully, and to touch, taste and listen to the world with soul. This is a significant step in, one that links what we thought about through our mindful exercises to a movement into soulful experience and expression.

Seeing from the soul!

So here's a simple but very significant way of getting us going, which involves seeing through the eyes of the soul.

You may not even have considered this until now, but when you manage to step back and notice your mind's anxious or insecure commentary – instead of just reacting automatically from it – then *who is doing the noticing*? If you're trying to pray, for instance, and you *notice* that thoughts have been distracting you (such noticing then enabling you to return to a place of stillness and prayer); or when you're lying in bed and you *notice* you've been worrying; or when you *notice* you've been fixating unnecessarily on your appearance after you glimpsed your reflection in a shop window; then who is doing the noticing?

It is a presence, a consciousness, that watches patiently from beyond the turbulence of the thinking mind, and to which we are able to return in those moments of realisation. The writer Eckhart Tolle calls it the 'witnessing presence', which is a lovely way of putting it. I believe this 'witnessing presence' is the soulful self. We usually mistake 'who we are' for the running commentary in our head, but this is not our true identity. We experience the true identity when we become aware, once more, of our own presence.

(If you struggle to think about yourself in terms of a presence, imagine for a moment that you are sitting with a friend or loved one who has just heard some terrible news. You are not able to fix or solve their problem, so all you can do – *all* you can do – is to sit with them, without speaking, and simply be. You are offering, in love, the very best of who you are, without trying to pose or pretend or prove anything; you can add no value except to give the gift of your presence, deeply and beautifully. This presence is with us, in fact, all the time, but usually we are not aware of it ourselves, as we are so caught up in the stream of words in our head.)

Tolle puts a name to the anxious ego – he calls it 'the Thinker' – and suggests that we can learn to 'watch the Thinker' from the perspective of the witnessing presence, and thus put distance between us and our anxious thoughts, which need not consume or drive us.

In so doing, I believe that we watch with the eyes of the soul – that assured and gentle presence that has been there all along. It is a beautiful, peaceful, joyful thing to sense that presence, and to realise that we *are* that presence. We inhabit that presence, or better still, we are inhabited *by* that presence.

And as a result, very practically, we can learn to see through fresh eyes.

For here's the thing: the 'witnessing presence' doesn't just have to be some kind of mindfulness tool that we use in order to keep witnessing the anxious thoughts in our mind alone – as if it's like a glorified closed-circuit TV system or security guard. If that's all we end up doing, we diminish the soulful self. Instead, as we keep watch through the eyes of the witnessing presence, we can lift our heads to witness the world around us, too – from the non-judgemental, compassionate and loving perspective of the soul.

Imagine!

This, then, is the moment when we can begin to see life differently; through *awakening* eyes, which aren't looking to judge narrowly what they see all the time and to pigeon-hole what they do and don't like, but through eyes that are opened, widely, with curiosity and appreciation, to witness and behold the very gift of life that is set before them, within the present moment.

Two practical exercises

So try this now (or as soon as you have a moment). Sit comfortably and close your eyes. Slow your breathing a little, and count ten breaths. As you do, gently notice any distractions or thoughts that enter your mind – 'watch the Thinker' without any judgement – but this time *experience* what it is like to be the witnessing presence, the one who is doing the watching.

And when you feel still, and ready, open your eyes and look around you: not through the eyes of the ego but of your soulful self. Try, very simply, to look upon all that is before you non-judgementally and with compassion and love.

Just observe. And enjoy.

When you look for the soul, you begin to look *from* the soul. And this is incredibly helpful practically, especially when it comes to relationships. I know how easy it is for me – by default – to look for what can be annoying about other people: to see their ego writ large, and to respond with mine. When you look with the eyes of the soul, you are able to begin to see past the ego in *other* people too, to their witnessing presence – and to remember that they are kindred souls, whether you like them or not.

A man told me the story of how he used to cross the road to avoid a certain elderly lady in the village where he lived; she was quite a difficult character and prone to speaking badly about people. He had been learning some mindfulness practice, however – in particular, simple meditation and breathing techniques, as we have already looked at – and the next time he saw her, he felt inspired to act differently. While his automatic impulse was still to cross the road, he over-rode the autopilot, choosing to stay where he was, and to speak to her.

Instead of reacting to her own insecurities, he wanted to engage from a position of assurance: to look for the soul in her from the perspective of the soul in him. So he connected lovingly, and asked her a few questions that focused on her, and which allowed her, quite soon, to express to him something of her love of the outdoors. She was going for a walk, and she was given space in the conversation to describe how much she loved being out in nature. They had what the man described as a 'soulful' conversation for over twenty minutes, then went on their way, both the better for it. It wasn't long after that that the old lady died – and the man felt grateful and inspired that he had been able to engage with her 'as deep calls to deep', to draw goodness from an otherwise awkward encounter, and to let soul connect with soul.

Soft eyes

Here is another practical exercise you can work with, called 'soft eyes'. Soft eyes helps us to look at the world in a different way to usual, developing a more soulful way of seeing.

Normally, we use what's known as our foveal vision – that is, a tiny area that is about 2.5mm wide on the retina. Foveal vision helps us to see details in a focused, analytical way – such as when we're trying to thread a needle, or to read a newspaper, or to look at a screen. (When we're looking at a screen 50cm away, our sharp field of foveal vision will be about 2.5cm in diameter.) Some people also refer to this way of looking as using 'hard eyes'. Foveal vision is about actively retrieving information through our eyes. It's great for detail, but too much of it and we can end up with eye strain, tension around the eyes, and tension further afield, such as in the jaw and shoulders. Of course, we use foveal vision when we are plugged into our electronic devices all day.

With 'soft eyes', we bring our much-neglected peripheral vision back into play. The aim is still to be able to see detail, but to maintain our wider field of vision, so that we are aware, in the moment, much more fully of what's around us. Soft eyes can be particularly useful in sport, for instance, and the best players will be able to receive a pass (focusing on the ball or puck) while sensing where everyone else is positioned on the field, in their periphery. It's also very useful for driving, when we need to be aware of what's to our left and right, and what's in the mirror, as well as what's in front of us.

Interestingly, hard eyes are associated with the beta state of consciousness, whereas with soft eyes we enter the alpha zone.

So this time, close your eyes, and when you are ready, open them without trying to focus on any one thing. Simply let the world *in* through your eyes. Your eyes are not focused on a particular object; they are simply open. Don't worry about whether you blink or not; you don't need to stare like a freak! Just look, with soft eyes. And stay with it for a few minutes if you can.

This mode of seeing is receptive ... you receive what you are seeing, and you are open to what you are seeing, in a non-judgemental way. It helps us to step into the world before us alert, awake and aware – but relaxed and compassionate, welcoming a world of mystery and grace that we might otherwise miss with hard eyes alone.

We are expanding our vision, widening our horizons, and all the while starting to see life again through the wondering eyes of the soulful self, which has been waiting so patiently all of this time to show us so much more.

You can use soft eyes as a daily discipline: stand in the garden or park for a few minutes and practise looking upon the world in this way. You might even combine it with the first exercise, becoming aware of the witnessing presence first, and then using soft eyes to see with the eyes of the soul. But when we remember that soulfulness is not disembodied, and that the soul senses the world around it, then the art of watching – for the soul and from the soul – is one that can be honed specifically using something as practical and physical as this soft eyes technique.

As we continue to work on this, the nature of the way we 'see' will shift. As Rod Windle and Suzanne Warren state (in a training manual written on conflict resolution for schools in the US, which uses this technique), 'Seeing in this way sends an entirely different set of signals to the brain from seeing with hard eyes. As our eyes see more, somehow our brains become more open to the diversity of possibilities that always surround us.' We become open to the world.

6

Sensing the soulful life

It's a profound thing to shift the way we see the world, and indeed to begin to see with the eyes of the soul. But this doesn't have to be restricted to sight alone, for each of our senses can help us to tune in to soul, and with soul – because soul, as we have said, is not detached from the physical realm, but fleshed out from within it.

Think about taste for a moment. What happens to you when you taste freshly picked fruit, in season, or vegetables grown from the local allotment (not flown half the way around the world); or when you have that first sip of a really special wine that a friend's been saving to share with you? Consider the blessing of a mouthful of water after you have been parched for too long on a hot day! A connection is made, which starts with the physical yet also somehow takes you beyond it;

there is alignment, in that soulful connection, between you and the world – and quite possibly the universe as well.

That's surely why it's soulful not to rush meals, but to savour each mouthful, and to share the experience if we can with family or friends.

Smell can also trigger a soulful response, can't it? Walk into a friend's house on a winter's day and smell a pot of fresh coffee and you're not just excited about the prospect of a delicious drink; somehow the atmosphere envelops you, lifts you into a different quality of space for a time. Perhaps you don't like coffee, but how about the smell of the salty sea as you step out of the car for the first time on arriving at the seaside after a long journey? Or the scent of woodland flowers carried on a warm evening's breeze in springtime?

We can use triggers such as smell to remind us to step back into that witnessing presence, and in that moment to relax, to give thanks, to remember we are here, and to bring that assured and peaceful presence to bear on the world around us.

Through touch, too, we can be taken to a different kind of place, right where we are. Whether it's a hand around our shoulder at a time of sadness, or the electricity of a first kiss, or even stroking a pet on our lap in front of a fire ... touch will reach beyond words and ego, through skin, right into your soul and mine; it is an extraordinary blessing when used in the appropriate context.

Imagine that feeling of cool water as you dive into a pool on a scorching hot afternoon, or a duvet that wraps itself snugly around you at the end of a difficult day, or a massage when you have a headache or stress-filled shoulders . . .

* * *

Our soul *senses*. I am sure of it. It sees, it tastes, it touches, it smells, it listens and it responds. I'd like to consider the art of listening now, as this can help us to listen for the whisper of our own soul, and also to listen *with* soul in order to bless others.

Good listening is not something, it seems, that we are taught or modelled very often, and so it's easy to go through life not realising how little we actually know about listening. (Sadly, today's generation is in particular danger of being raised by parents who are more tuned in to their phones than to their children.) Perhaps we notice as we get older that our hearing is suffering – but what about the quality of our *listening*, however old we are?

According to the doctor, pastor and author Russ Parker, an expert in the art of listening, there are a few common pitfalls when it comes to listening, several of which I can identify with.

We can start mentally juggling thoughts as we try to listen, getting distracted with our to-do list in particular and losing focus.

We can be impatient, wanting to hurry people on to the point of what they are saying, and giving off non-verbal cues that will be picked up by the person we're listening to, whether we try to hide them or not. (How does it feel when you are being hurried up like this? What effect does it have on the nature of what you are willing to disclose?)

We can also rehearse what we are going to say next (it's that moment when someone says, 'Oh, that happened to me . . .' – and you realise they haven't been listening at all, but waiting to jump in with their own story).

We can start trying to fix someone's problem, and so we stop focusing on what they are actually trying to tell us, and concentrate instead on our own solution. Most of the time, people are telling us something in order simply to be heard, not to have their problems solved (whichever our gender!).

And finally, we can (perhaps worst of all!) go into pretend-mode, trying to look as if we're interested, when really we're not.

I wonder if you're a juggler, a hurry-upper, a rehearser, a fixer or a pretender? Perhaps you are several, like me. But don't despair – becoming aware of these pitfalls is more than half the battle, because you are then better placed to *notice* when you've fallen into one of them, before returning to a place of stillness and awareness and focusing on the other person.

Now that we have identified some of these pitfalls, let's consider three levels at which we can listen or 'tune in' to others.

First, there is conversational listening, which oils the wheels of a relationship but may not touch on matters that are too deep. A friendly chat at a restaurant with friends on a fun evening out may require conversational listening in order to keep the flow and keep it fun.

Deeper below that level is what we call active listening. This is when we listen in order specifically to get information or to tune in more intentionally. Active listening requires that we tune out other 'noise' and focus in harder and more attentively, and sometimes this means taking notes.

But then, one level further in, is *deep* listening. This is what we do when we shut out everything else, and it's almost as if there is no one but you and the person you are listening to in the whole world. But here's the thing: you don't just listen actively, you listen in a way that goes beyond words themselves – empathetically, yes, but also soulfully.

You may have engaged in this kind of listening without realising it, perhaps when a friend shared some awful news with you about a scary medical diagnosis, for instance, or a relationship breakdown. Suddenly you are 'there' with them so much more fully than you'd normally have been, and you are both tuned in to each other at a profound level. It is as though you have taken to another place together, even though you haven't moved, and you are sharing the same space: soul space, where there is a meeting of souls. Another example

83

would be when you are falling in love, and you have eyes for absolutely no one and nothing else.

Of course, you cannot maintain the deepest form of listening for ever; it takes energy and work and skill. There'll be times when a cosmetic or conversational approach is indeed entirely appropriate. But there will be other times when you have the opportunity to give someone else the gift of deep listening, which will help them to feel as if they have been properly heard, for perhaps the first time in their life. (Russ Parker believes that listening is the most effective remedy for conflict, particularly when the person doing the talking senses that they have truly been heard.)

Now, this is a soulful approach in itself, to offer someone the gift of active or deep listening. However, we can extend this out to the way we listen in any situation – not just to a friend or work colleague, for instance, but to the world around us in all its complex and greater wholeness. This includes listening to nature (which we'll consider in depth soon), and listening to your self.

As we listen *for* the soul, we are able then to listen from the soul.

A quick recap on the journey so far

Let's trace the journey we've been on so far, before we continue. From time to time, we glimpse tantalising moments of soulfulness, but for much of the time, the soul can be drowned out by the chatter of the ego, and smothered by the masks we wear and the personas we adopt to stay safely out of reach and never too vulnerable.

When we engage in contemplative spiritual disciplines or mindful practice, we allow our often anxious and insecure minds to find stillness at last, which can bring deep rest and relief from our striving.

But within that stillness, we are able to discover not just the absence of noise, but the intriguing presence of something that is not the noise. The presence of soul. These can be profound glimpses of awakening, but often we step back from them, choosing to re-enter our busyness or 'mediocrity and escapism' because we are fearful of the consequences of pursuing a more soulful path – or we simply can't imagine living differently.

But we have a choice, both within our more intentional times of awakening, and also when we are caught by surprise by an unexpectedly soulful connection – with nature, or God, or someone else, or with our self . . . At those times, we have the choice to press 'further up and further in' to the soulful life, by tuning in proactively to the soul's leading, and, if you like, to befriend it. To welcome who we truly are, perhaps even for the first time.

We cannot dissect our soul, but we *can* watch for it, and listen for it, and sense its presence. And as we do – as we reach in *for* our soul – we can begin to reach out *from* our soul, to the world around us.

7

Meeting your self, as if for the first time

While the witnessing presence, our soulful self, waits patiently for us to awaken, it is not, however, in some pious and passive religious state. The soul in you longs to run free and to find expression and explore the untrodden paths of your life, your world! It is dynamic, energetic, fulfilling, and larger than (your hitherto limited) life.

I'd like to offer a few simple ways now of helping us to welcome, and to become reacquainted with and then to befriend the soul, so that we are able to enter the world of risk, and colour, and daring, and imagination, and wonder, and passion. It takes practice recognising when the soul stirs, then it takes courage to act upon that stirring, but as we learn to welcome the soul we can also learn to live with soul.

Here are a few ways to start fleshing out the idea of soul in our lives.

1. Put yourself in a position where you know your soul will stir!

One positive way to identify and begin to befriend soul is to look proactively for the times when your soul stirs – and to see what happens when it does.

That might be when you get outside into nature, for instance, and smell the forest pine, or freshly cut grass; it might be when you listen to some 'soulful' music, and find yourself in thrall to the rhythm and being lifted, somehow; or when you are watching an inspiring film, and your horizons are widening and your vision expanding. We've all been in that soulful zone and we know what it's like to sense that deeper connection between the outside and the inside of our life. It's a great thing.

We'll consider a little further on what feeds the soul, but for now simply consider: where do you go, or what do you like to do, to feel your soul stir? When you next have the chance, go there. But why not, in the meantime, sit quietly, pause, and go back there in your mind's eye right now. What is it that you love about where you find yourself? How are your senses heightened or activated? What can you see, hear, touch, taste, smell? What is the nature of the connection between the unique 'aliveness' within you and the 'aliveness' of what lies beyond you? How does this connection make you feel, and how do you tend to respond?

*   *   *

Intriguingly, we can often feel a sense of accompanying melancholy, or dissatisfaction, arising at these soulful times, because we know the connection rarely seems to last; we're in touch with something magical, and we sense that there must be – and surely is! – more to life than our own petty concerns and selfish narrative. But then it slips away; and in its place we feel an aching and a longing. The moment is lost, almost before it has begun, and the magic has only served to highlight the mundanity of busyness-as-usual.

For this reason, one thing we often do instinctively is to try to 'capture' the moment with a photograph, using our phone or camera. A quick scroll through your picture files will show you perhaps a few times when you have indeed tried to do just that; most likely, you didn't succeed anyway (it's almost impossible to ever fully do *that* moment justice) and instead you've ended up merely 'watching' the scene on your phone's screen, instead of being there. You missed it before you experienced it.

So for a change, and as something of a discipline, leave your phone or camera in your pocket next time you encounter a truly soulful situation, and stay intentionally *within* the scene itself. You may find it helpful, when you are tempted to whip out the camera, to return your attention deliberately to your breathing instead (to count ten breaths, perhaps) – in order, intentionally, to welcome your soul to the surface, and to let *it* become the one who is breathing in the beauty of this present moment, slowly and deeply.

Stay there awhile, not trying to capture anything, but being there more fully within it all. Watching with the eyes of the soul.

I have found when I'm leading outdoor retreats that some of the most helpful times of awakening arrive for people when they begin to accept – sometimes for the first time – that they are a natural part of what they see around them. It's easy for us to stand back, especially in a beautiful setting, and admire (for instance) a lovely garden or woodland or landscape. It's quite another thing to accept that we are part of that very loveliness itself, reflecting something unique about the beauty of the world simply through being there, fully present.

So you can try this, too. Find a place to be, and look around you. Appreciate what you can see. Now, picture yourself within the scene. You might imagine looking from above, or from a few steps back, behind or to the side of you. See yourself standing there, not through the eyes of the ego – wondering what other people might be thinking of you, or whether your clothes look good, and so on – but through the compassionate eyes of the soul. See yourself as a work of art, a work of creation, a fully organic part of the landscape, as much as any beautiful tree or flower or river. And continue to watch yourself for a few minutes, allowing feelings of compassion and love to flow. This is part of the act of 'giving flesh-and-blood expression' to your unique inner aliveness. If you see yourself as part of the beauty of the scene, you no longer have to compete, or compare, or control from the ego. Instead, you give expression to soul, and your very presence can inspire others to do likewise.

* * *

You don't have to restrict this practice to a landscape, though it's a good place to start. You can also become part of the beauty of the scene *wherever* you find yourself. This could mean within the open-plan office, for instance. Try if you can to picture yourself, once more, within the scene, and imagine giving expression beautifully, through being your assured and soulful self, within that context. You may need to work slightly harder to see beauty within an office setting, but look for it and it will be there, within the people, and their work, and their relationships.

I've also found this to be a helpful exercise within a sea of shoppers on the high street!

2. Loving-kindness exercise

We've noted already that we don't possess soul, like a commodity; if anything, it's the other way round! One helpful way to experience and to welcome soul is through a simple yet powerful and popular form of meditation which allows 'loving-kindness' to flow within us, before directing it out to the world around us. In so doing, I have found that we become better able to accept ourselves, and to welcome more of our soulful self.

Loving-kindness is a delightful term that courses through Christianity, Judaism and Buddhism in particular. It was 'coined' in the Coverdale translation of the Bible in 1535 as a translation of the Hebrew word *chesed*, a term that is often found in the Psalms (but also elsewhere) and which refers to acts of kindness motivated by love (and God's love in particular). In Buddhism, the term *metta* refers to benevolence or compassion: a love without condition or expectation.

In a loving-kindness meditation, we start by focusing inwards on ourselves, because it's hard to extend love or kindness out to others until and unless we can first apply it to our own self.

It's very hard to even consider ourselves worthy of receiving loving-kindness without hearing that chattering voice in our head begin to complain: 'I can't love myself – that's selfish!' or 'I am unworthy of love' or 'What's going to happen if I do?' But when those thoughts arise, you can smile gently, with compassion, and breathe, and relax, and return to a place of soulful acceptance.

And so, very simply: as you sit quietly, and take a few deeper breaths, allow feelings of kindness and love to flow towards you, let yourself smile, and wish yourself well.

You might like to imagine yourself as a child who is fully deserving of love (even if you didn't receive as much as you'd have liked when you were young); hold that child in your loving attention. Let feelings of peace and joy well up within you. (You might also note the contrast between these feelings and what was there before, such as tension, fear, uptightness, judgemental-ism.) This is a soulful place in which to find yourself, and to be still – as yourself.

Personally, I also find it hugely helpful to imagine seeing myself through God's eyes – as I believe that God loves me unconditionally. You might like to try that as an alternative, and receive the loving-kindness that flows from deep within as a result.

Kathleen Grace-Bishop, of the University of New Hampshire Health Services, suggests in a very helpful online version of the meditation that we repeat the following words slowly and purposefully to ourselves, for as long as we need:

May I be well,
may I be happy,
may I be peaceful,
may I be loved.

Stay in that flow for as long as you want, before imagin-ing loving-kindness beginning to flow out from you to those around you. You can, of course, try this anywhere – you don't need to be in a quiet place; a crowded train is just as appropriate!

Loving-kindness for others

As we reach in for soul, we can reach out soulfully to the world around us.

So, we can extend the loving-kindness meditation we practised for our self in order to hold others, too, in our awareness and attention with loving-kindness. In fact, this can become a most beautiful form of prayer beyond words, whether you are used to praying or not.

Sitting quietly, repeat the loving-kindness meditation, and once you have entered that flow of loving-kindness, allow your attention to turn to a friend, colleague, family member, or even someone who has wronged you. Imagine them sitting in front of you. You may even be in the same room as them, and wish to use this as a way of sending them love. You may be sitting next to a stranger on the bus. Let kindness and love flow out to them from deep within you; cradle them in your own soulful awareness and attention, and wish them well. Try using Kathleen Grace-Bishop's words once more, but this time saying,

> May you be well,
> may you be happy,
> may you be peaceful,
> may you be loved.

I have found this to be a very moving process, and one that helps me tune in to the soul of the other person, instead of fixating on the reactive nature of their own often anxious and insecure ego.

I tried this recently with a man who had been deliberately dishonest with me. It felt unsettling at first to wish him well, but as I settled in to the process, I slowly began to see his soul from my soul, and it helped me to put into practice the words of Jesus that I have hitherto struggled to embody: 'Love your enemies, and pray for those who persecute you.' *Wish him well*. This really does help us to establish in our hearts a deeper and more gracious connection that also allows for the flow of forgiveness and acceptance.

Relationship becomes about far, far more than what we can get out of it. And this takes us far beyond establishing a coping strategy in a stressful world; it's about a courageous determination to re-establish a flow of self-giving love, by breaking a vicious cycle and establishing some form of loving reconnection. This is not easy, of course – humility, grace and kindness all require that we stand down our selfish pride and become willing to be the one to offer the hand of love and friendship first. Another crack appears in the shiny surface of the ego when we do this, which is painful; so it requires courage to continue with it. But it just so happens that when we release the flow of loving-kindness, it's as good for our own soul as it for those we are seeking to benefit.

3. Recognise when you don't act from ego for a change

Perhaps you were caught up in an argument and were faced with a difficult, argumentative or aggressive person, and instead of reacting in kind, for a change you were able, with calmness, to absorb their anger, and to respond by pouring peace, not petrol, onto an otherwise combustible situation. You may well have surprised yourself by the strength that arose within you during that moment; you caught a glimpse of soul, and so did the person for whom you showed compassion.

Or you may have faced a work situation, and rather than being braced for what might go wrong – body tense, mind whirring – perhaps you found yourself, to your surprise, to be relaxed and present, within the moment, and you felt a sense of flow with your surroundings. During these moments, we may feel as if we have nothing to prove, or little to gain, for a change; and instead of shifting our shape for others, we end up helping to set the tone by being more fully ourselves, in a benevolent and loving way. Ask yourself:

What was I doing?
How was I acting?
What was different from usual?

Try, with the next person you meet or the next situation you encounter, to be more intentionally relaxed, undefended and open. You may find it helpful to bring your attention to your breathing, just before you step into the situation, in order to calm your mind and become present. You may find it helpful, as an abbreviated version of the loving-kindness exercise, to pause, to consider the people you are about to meet, and to wish them well. You might also, in a moment's preparation, ask yourself the counter-cultural question 'What can go right?' instead of wrong! This will help you to look for what's good, and instead of approaching with caution, you can step in with openness, and love, and a willingness to serve.

4. Call your name

When it comes to welcoming and befriending your own soul, here's one further short exercise you can try, which is quite fun but also profound, and helps you to 'wake up' to your self by calling your own name. You may feel slightly silly doing this, but it can be both moving and significant, so let's give it a try.

Sit in a quiet room with the door closed, preferably at home, and make sure you have a few minutes when you will not be interrupted. Make yourself comfortable. Close your eyes, and bring your attention to your breath. Relax, and pause for a short while.

When you are ready, say your own name, gently and compassionately. Leave a gap of five seconds or so, and repeat. Keep doing this for a few minutes, over and over.

You'll find, before long, that it feels as if someone else is calling you. It's as if someone is waking you up. As this happens, invite your soul to respond to the call. Allow your soulful self some time and space just to be.

Once you've finished the exercise, proceed into the next part of your day seeking to respond soulfully instead of reacting anxiously to whatever you face next.

*　　*　　*

You never know: you might actually be surprised by who you really are. We spend so much of our time trying to second-guess other people's expectations of who we should be that we get caught up in trying to fulfil those hypothetical expectations, instead of learning more about what makes us 'us'.

Soul expresses itself in the smallest of ways

If you've ever been in love, you'll remember how, with senses heightened and heart racing, you couldn't help noticing and celebrating some of the smallest details about the object of your love: their mannerisms, their idiosyncrasies, their foibles – and it's likely that you cherished that person all the more *because* of them.

She might love the way he laughs, for instance, or how he always stops to listen to buskers, or makes a point of saying hello to complete strangers. He can't help it. He just does it.

97

He might adore the way she dances when she thinks no one is watching, or the way she speaks to animals as if they were people, or turns her face to the sun when it finally comes out from behind the clouds, closing her eyes to soak up the warmth and the light like a flower in bloom.

I wonder what you have appreciated about someone else. What have you seen in them that perhaps no one else has seen in quite the same way, and which speaks of their soul?

And what has someone seen in you? For it takes the appreciation of a friend or a loved one to help us to realise *our* own uniqueness in turn.

Over time, perhaps, we grow a little too familiar with these small, soulful details, and we might stop noticing them in quite the same way. Nevertheless, they remain part of each of us, beautiful, particular, *witnessed*. And they matter, too, simply because someone has awoken to the way your soul finds expression. Someone you might call your soul friend.

*　　*　　*

Years later, there may come a time when those smallest soulful mannerisms start to matter again more dramatically than ever before. We will, one day, have to say goodbye, whether that's through break-up or through death. Either can leave us acutely bereft.

Isn't it interesting, though, how when a friend, family member or partner dies, we seem to reflect back on

98

their life with even greater attention to those smaller details? Somehow, instinctively, we *know* that these were what set them apart, not the stand-out grandiose moments from their CV. We celebrate the gorgeously simple, outward and (so frequently) physical manifestations of their inner life, their soul, which brought them alive to *us* and expressed their one-of-a-kind-ness to the world.

And we see, sometimes with greater clarity and perspective, how their soul has walked with us, danced with us, stared out to sea with us . . . found expression with us, and touched our soul in the process.

It makes me want to savour the seemingly insignificant ways of my friends and family while I still have them, and while they still have me. Wouldn't it be lovely if we could all release each other to relax, to be more fully ourselves, and to bring both our idiosyncrasies and our gifts to bear on all that we do? To express with greater confidence through our life today what people will eventually come to acknowledge in their eulogy upon our death?

The mystery of how soul connects the eternal to the everyday

We see the soul expressed in the smallest, loveliest gestures of a person's life, yet it's also the soul that links us to the infinite, as John O'Donohue reminds us. At a funeral, my Christian faith gives me hope that the soul will not perish. So for me soul is like a gateway between the everyday and the eternal, and this has implications for both.

First, it means that I can be mindful of bringing a sense of the eternal – that there is a bigger picture, and we are part of a greater unfolding story! – to even the most mundane of situations I face. Instead of going through the motions at a business meeting, for instance, or even (dare I say) with my kids at the park, if I am able to see through the eyes of the soul, and to step back into my own soulful presence (instead of being caught up in ego, distracted and absent), then I can imbue the present moment with 'more'. Just as the appearance of a rainbow lifts and inspires and reconnects us, so also can the presence of a woman or man who is 'linked into the infinite', and who knows they are part of something greater.

Second, the nature of soul changes the way we can view 'heaven'. Because if soul is expressed so frequently in the smallest flesh-and-blood ways we do things, creatively and in love, and if soul survives death, then it suggests to me that we won't be floating on clouds in eternity so much as continuing to give profound *flesh-and-blood* expression to our unique, inner aliveness instead! 'In heaven, as it was on Earth', to turn the words of the Lord's Prayer around for a moment.

Personally, I savour the words of Jesus, who told his followers shortly before he was arrested, 'I will not drink from this fruit of the vine from now on until that

day when I drink it new with you in my Father's kingdom'. He was planning to sit down with them and drink
wine in eternity, it seems. That's a vision that fills me
with hope.

The physical resurrection of Jesus went on to point
to a different idea of eternity than the one we so often
imagine, reminding us as well that the Bible speaks of
'new heavens and a new *earth*' in the age to come. This,
of course, is a mystery that we cannot hope to grasp
fully – but for me it transforms the idea of the next life
being like a retirement home for vicars, and promises,
instead, another physical adventure. 'God will give life
to your mortal bodies,' Paul assures us.

On one occasion when Jesus appeared to his followers in the flesh after his death and resurrection, he ate a
breakfast of fish on the beach with them. Now, if this
wasn't a soulful encounter – linking the infinite so
magnificently with the humanity of sharing a meal with
friends, on a *beach* of all places! – then surely nothing is.

In this one encounter, we glimpse how soul connects
who we are now (like the disciples) with who we will be
(like the risen Christ). Jesus was still Jesus, though he
was transformed. And all of the indescribable cosmic
mystery that is contained in the themes of life and death,
soul and body, happens over breakfast. This biblical
vignette, then, helps me not just to find huge excitement
about the nature of the life to come, but to see that we
can start to embody the 'more' of that promise soulfully
in the life we have now.

In the sharing of breakfast on a beach.
In the gathering of souls round the fire.

* * *

I adore the idea that the physical blessings of life continue to be shared in what we would otherwise consider to be the 'spiritual' realm! And as for wine and fish breakfasts, so too – surely? – for all the soul-affirming wonders of the physical realm of creation, such as music and art and nature. Why not?

So I wonder, what piece of music would you like to be played at your funeral?

How would it remind those in attendance about the nature of your soul?

And imagine – just imagine – if it were playing in your honour as you were welcomed into the physical realm of eternity! What would it tell the people *there* about who they could expect to meet?

8

Sharpening the focus on our uniqueness – some questions to ponder

In Part 2, we've been 'reaching in' to consider what our unique, inner aliveness might be like, and to glimpse more of who we were created to be. In Part 3, we'll ask how we can reach *out* through soul . . . in particular, to each other, to God and to nature, but more generally to Life itself!

But to end our reflections on 'reaching in', I'd like to ask a few simple but significant questions associated with the derivations of the word *nephesh* I mentioned at the start of Part 2, which will help you to sharpen the focus of your own unique, inner aliveness. How are *you* unique, and how can you bring such uniqueness to bear, as gift, to the world around you?

You may like to take each of these carefully and reflectively, and spend time pondering them; alternatively, you may prefer to answer spontaneously without too much thought. Both processes have their place.

So, then:

(a) If soul is a **living being**, what brings you to life?

   When do you really come alive in a positive and meaningful way? Is it in the surf on a blowy spring evening? Is it painting a water-colour picture of a cloudscape? Is it playing in an orchestra, or making pilgrimage, or going for a run, or . . .?

   What have you reflected upon in Part 2 about 'reaching in' that helps you to understand more about the distinctiveness of your own soul? And in what ways would it benefit you, and the world around you, if you were able to come alive more often?

(b) If soul is **life itself**, how does it find expression through you?

   What are the small but individual ways of doing things that might be remembered by others at your own funeral? How do you think you bring life to those around you, and thus bring those around you to life? And how do you help to inspire and challenge those around you through 'who you are' – your presence – as much as through what you do? When do you notice people specifically

drawing energy and inspiration from you, and
what does this tell you about who you are and
what more you can offer to the world through
acting from the soul?

(c) If soul is a **person**, who is the real you?

It's a big, big question, but have a look in the
mirror, and remember that you are not a body with
a soul, but you are the soul. We can spend a life-
time reaching in for soul, and it's a mysterious and
enigmatic pursuit, but what hints and glimpses of
the 'real' *you* might you have gleaned from the
exercises so far?

(d) If soul is **desire**, what do you long for most truly?

It's not about wishing life were different – wishing is usually a waste of time, because it doesn't get
us anywhere! But what do you yearn for in a positive and healthy way? Perhaps you quietly hope to
find a job that fits more happily with your own
gifts and strengths, for instance. Sometimes, the
soul is stirring us, nudging us to contemplate
making a move, doing something different, trying
something new. Have you sensed a positive desire
stirring in you, one that you can take a step or two
practically towards?

(e) If soul is **passion**, what are you fighting for?

Let's remember that soul is not a passive or
pious state of equilibrium. It is right to be
passionate, and to notice what you are passionate about. What are you fighting positively for

in life? What's stopping you from doing something about it? What is it that you truly stand for, and how can the courage of your convictions be manifested through the choices you make *today*?

(f) If soul is **appetite**, what do you hunger and thirst for?

Perhaps you have been lacking soulful nourishment in recent days. We will explore the nature of 'soul food' in Part 4, when we ask how to form soulful rhythms in which you take energy in, as well as give energy out. But for now, think about the quality of what you've been feeding yourself recently – whether that's literally or figuratively – and consider whether you're hungering or thirsting to do something you'd consider to be good for your soul: for instance, to go for a walk at the seaside, or to make time for watching a play or an opera, or to catch a film that will inspire or challenge you positively. You'll know what really feeds you, if you pause to consider it – and this will help you to become better aware of your soulful self.

(g) If soul is **emotion**, what are your feelings teaching you?

Some people find it helpful to 'review' their day before they go to bed, using an exercise introduced by St Ignatius known as the Examen. The Examen has five gentle but purposeful steps. They vary slightly, depending on which books you read, but they can be summed up broadly as:

1. Pause to be still, and become aware of God's presence.
2. Review the day with gratitude.
3. Pay attention to the emotions that you experienced throughout the day.
4. Choose one feature of the day and pray about it.
5. Look forward to tomorrow.

The priest and author Mark Thibodeaux, in his book *Reimagining the Ignatian Examen*, explains how he approaches step 3, by reviewing the different emotions he has experienced in the day, before choosing the strongest one and noticing the impact it has had upon him. 'Did I even acknowledge the emotion as I experienced it,' he asks, 'or was I unaware of it? Did I consciously choose how to act on this emotion, or did I allow the emotion to choose how I would think, speak and act throughout the day?'

The writer and theologian Frederich Buechner emphasises throughout his inspiring books the importance of 'listening to your life', and he says we can do this in many ways, including paying careful attention to our emotions. But here's a lovely thing, in particular, to watch for and to give your attention to: unexpected tears.

'You never know what may cause them,' he writes.

The sight of the Atlantic Ocean can do it, or a piece of music, or a face you've never seen before. A pair of somebody's old shoes can do it ... You can never be sure. But of this you can be sure. Whenever you find tears in your eyes, especially unexpected tears, it is well to pay the closest attention. They are not only telling you something about the secret of who you are, but more often than not God is speaking to you ...

*   *   *

What Buechner describes with unexpected tears is a tender moment of awakening. It happened to me once at a wildlife sanctuary in France, which staged a bird display so jaw-dropping – clouds of birds were flying all around the audience, synchronised to music, in a way that I can't possibly begin to describe adequately – that my only response was through tear-filled eyes. Something was happening to me beyond my immediate comprehension; a sense of stirring, and connection, and love, and reawakening, that was indescribable. As with all such moments, we have a choice: ignore or neglect them through our unawareness, or notice them, and by contemplating them further, allow them to speak into us.

Perhaps, then, to conclude Part 2, you could consider any similar moments of awakening that you have experienced recently, which you may otherwise have missed.

One of the best known parables of Jesus, the Parable of the Sower, very helpfully reminds us of the abundance of seeds of awakening that are scattered throughout our life. The question is, how can we help them to fall into good soil, take root and grow?

A farmer went out to sow his seed. As he was scattering the seed, some fell along the path, and the birds came and ate it up. Some fell on rocky places, where it did not have much soil. It sprang up quickly, because the soil was shallow. But when the sun came up, the plants were scorched, and they withered because they had no root. Other seed fell among thorns, which grew up and choked the plants. Still other seed fell on good soil, where it produced a crop – a hundred, sixty or thirty times what was sown.

Every day we receive all sorts of hints that there is more to life than first meets the eye. Seeds of soulful awakening, we could call them. As we spend a few minutes in stillness, or take a walk, or even just pause to count ten breaths, we become better placed to *receive* the gifts that were waiting here for us all along, in the present – and to notice the path that emerges from out of the fog of our busyness, and that invites us to step out purposefully onto it in pursuit of a greater adventure. Just as every seed has the potential to grow and to produce a crop, so too every human life has the potential to flourish.

Part 3

Reaching out with soul: reconnecting lovingly with all parts of life

9

Soul friendship

In Part 3, we consider what it means to reach out to the world around us through soul, which is not only distinctive, but truly connective.

And one of the ways to reach out is through *soul friendship*.

I don't just mean romantically (although plenty of people describe their partners as their 'soul mate', and this is a delightful thing); but *any* friendship has the potential for one soul to call to another from beyond the transactional and cursory nature of so many of our casual or snatched acquaintanceships.

Life *is* busy, and it's easy to skim the surface of our relationships, especially when we rely on social media to keep us updated with what's going on in each other's lives. But there is far more to life beneath the surface of our 'status updates', as we all know, and while not everyone we meet will be destined to be a soul friend, nevertheless, if we watch carefully, we can always find soulful ways to connect more fully and deeply with anyone we are blessed enough to encounter in our everyday life.

So what does soul friendship involve?

Here, I return to John O'Donohue for help, who explains that the Gaelic term for soul friend is *anam cara* (such a gorgeous-sounding phrase in itself!). *Anam cara*, he tells us, originally referred to someone to whom you could make confession, and with whom you could share the hidden intimacies and secrets of your life.

When we are able to reveal something of our innermost self, we find both recognition (someone else can see us more truly for who we are) and belonging. And delightfully (though unsurprisingly), the soul connection transcends all social conventions and expectations, for *anam cara* is ultimately, as O'Donohue affirms, about 'a deep and special companionship'.

Perhaps you can bring someone to mind who has offered you this kind of companionship. We don't always recognise it as such at the time, of course, or receive it as such, or nurture it as fully as we could. (Is someone offering you soul friendship at the moment, but you are too distracted to notice?)

Sometimes companionships like this begin to suffer if they are too one-sided or we take them for granted instead of treasuring them. The deep and special friendships in our life also have the capacity to hurt us the most if and when they do go wrong. Yet think for a moment about someone who really has been a true companion, and consider what you have released and inspired in each other because of your friendship.

It may only have been for a season, but what would not have been born or made manifest without a meeting of your souls?

* * *

When it comes to soul friends, I'm reminded of my wife's grandmother, Patricia. She was born into a successful family from Nottingham, and grew up in pretty high society. During the Second World War Patricia was brought back from finishing school in Switzerland to help with the war effort, and was posted as a WREN in Portsmouth, the strategic naval port in the south of England, where she worked in the evenings as a projectionist at the local cinema. She was assigned a chaperone to escort her back to barracks safely after dark, and this turned out to be a rough-hewn northern Irishman called Mick, a fisherman who had joined the navy. Mick was convalescing in Portsmouth, having survived the sinking of his aircraft carrier the HMS *Glorious*. Only thirty men were pulled alive from the icy North Sea when it was sunk by enemy gunfire – three days after it had sunk – out of the 1200 on board. He was as tough as old boots, and utterly unsuitable for Patricia in terms of class and background. And yet ...

the two fell for each other, coming to love each other deeply: it was as if they had been made for each other. Mick had to wait for six long and frustrating years before he was fully and finally accepted by Patricia's family and they could marry, but both were determined to stay the course: nothing would keep them apart, and, in the end, nothing did. Patricia was freed from the life-limiting constraints of social convention and Mick was freed to be himself. Life went on to throw many great challenges at them, including the acute post-traumatic effects of Mick's rescue, and the loss of their son, aged nineteen, in a motor accident. But they remained devoted soul friends until the day Mick died. Patricia would sometimes talk, into her older age, of longing to 'go home' to be reunited with Mick. I love to believe that when finally shes died, they were indeed reunited – and to imagine those two souls finding each other once more.

*   *   *

'When you really feel understood,' writes O'Donohue, 'you feel free to release your self into the trust and shelter of the other person's soul.' Isn't it a blessed relief to find that you *can* trust and be trusted in this often fraught and suspicious world? It is rare but energising and heartening to discover that you can relate without judgement or pressure. We find rest when we take shelter in another's *soul*; and the contrast between this sense of rest and the daily, draining jostle of egos becomes ever more apparent. Give me shelter, any time.

And this kind of relational space is not just restorative but transformational, because as we enter it, we gain permission to pause from trying to prove ourselves, one ego to another, to start relating instead as one soul to another – in all our true distinctiveness – with great assurance. The power of this simply cannot be underestimated, for it is where something as yet unknown can be revealed; for as soul calls to soul, we glimpse more of each other's deeper identity, and are thus better able to bear witness to what has lain unwitnessed, and to help nurture the distinct soulful identity that lies within each other.

In this way, a soul friend can help me to discover more about myself, even as I discover more about them. The circle does indeed become a virtuous one.

* * *

Soul friendship takes us beyond the normal expectations of what you can do for me, and what I can do for you, therefore. It leads us deeper into the mystery of meeting your true self with my true self. And even if it's not two-way, there are practical reasons why it pays to engage soulfully with the world and the people around us. When we act from the ego, we usually get a *re*action from the other ego(s) involved. So we get stuck in a loop. We might all be seeking to impress, or to pretend we are OK when we're not. No one wants to blink first, because we're all afraid of being found out. In the office, who wants to leave their desk first when it's time to go home?

If you've been caught in a road rage incident you'll know what it's like to get stuck in a loop, and it can all happen in the blink of an eye (or the shake of a fist). Someone cuts you up with some terrible driving, you're incensed and flash your lights, they gesture back with their hand, you return the gesture with interest, they slam on their brakes ... It's how fights start, and it's how wars continue.

It's far harder to respond from soul, so don't let anyone tell you that this is somehow a tree-huggers' way to go. It's the narrowest path, it's the one we continually forget is even there, yet the most powerful option is to follow the soul's lead. This may take some doing: returning to your breathing within the heat of the moment, noticing your ego's reaction, letting that go – it all takes practice – yet when we manage it, in the midst of the action, we call out the best, or at least the better, in the others involved, and break the ego-to-ego feedback loop that is potentially so destructive.

It takes greatest courage to respond from the soul when your ego is being threatened, because the ego is so used to defending you and returning fire through words or gestures or actions. Let the soul lead, however, by giving the very best of yourself, your *nephesh*, to the situation, and in particular to the person in front of you, and you will change the tone of your engagement and the quality of the day.

*   *   *

We cannot all be soul friends; most of us look on enviously when people truly believe they have found one. A relationship like Patricia and Mick's is rare. Yet we can surely nurture the soulfulness of our relationships to bring a little more soul to bear.

You can sit in silence because you do not need to fill the space.

You can share a deep experience.

You can learn not to defend yourself incessantly, and instead be positively vulnerable.

You can bring your very best to bear on any situation, not just the good ones.

You can change the mood of a day, or the quality of an atmosphere, simply by choosing to respond with assurance, freedom and love.

And while we may not, at this moment, enjoy a depth of relationship with a particular special companion – someone with whom we can share our innermost self, and to whom we can be entirely vulnerable and honest – nevertheless, as O'Donohue stunningly concludes: God can be *anam cara* to each of us: a friend who (as the Bible describes it) is 'closer than a brother'.

Consider this, therefore: that at the very deepest and most sacred and hidden point of your being, the most intimate friendship of all is possible.

10

Connecting with God

You don't *have* to believe in God to believe you have a soul, of course, nor to live a soulful life; but I think it's very hard to speak of soul without at least considering its connection to the divine. The Franciscan monk and writer Richard Rohr has a clear and creative definition of soul, which helps me to understand more about this dynamic friendship which lies at the very heart of life. Ultimately, Fr Rohr says, the soul is who I am in God, and who God is in me. 'The self-same moment that we find God in ourselves,' he writes, 'we also find ourselves in God.'

I used to be one of those people who believe that connecting with God is about having some kind of telephone hot-line ... and it always felt frustrating or bewildering if God didn't seem to be answering it.

Richard Rohr's definition of soul helps me instead to see the connection as more of an interface between the human and the divine, a place where there is no boundary between us. It is 'both/and': God is in me, and I am in God. The apostle Paul (in his letter to the Colossians) refers to 'this mystery, which is Christ in you, the hope of glory'.

When I ponder this further, I find it, helpfully, *mysteriously* hard to imagine, at the deepest level of who I am, where 'Christ' ends and I begin; or where what's divine becomes what's human, and what's human becomes divine. It truly *is* a mystery, and certainly one that cannot be solved by dissection. Deep within me, deep within you, the divine and the human meet.

If Richard Rohr is right, what could this mean for us practically? Perhaps, to start with, we may acknowledge that our life is indeed sacred; that we are not simply isolated units imposing our will upon the world around us, but that we share together in the sacredness of life itself.

We are in God and God is in us.
We are in life, and life is in us.
We are in love, and love is in us.

That's not to say that religion always, or indeed often, gets it right; I have been to enough soulless services to know that 'religious' does not necessarily or automatically equate to 'soulful'. If we are not open to mystery, then religion can become dogmatic and demoralising. (On the other hand, if we are so anti-religious that we refuse the possibility of cohering with the divine, then I believe we diminish ourselves in a similar way.) Wherever we stand, it is perhaps the very act of staying open to this deeper connection with God, life and love that also deepens the soulful connection between us.

Mother Teresa once said, 'I see God in every human being. When I wash the leper's wounds I feel I am nursing the Lord himself. Is it not a beautiful experience?'

Can I see the divine in you?

Can you see the divine in me?

In a sense, of course, we have to make a rational decision: I *will* look for the divine in this person, even if the divine doesn't seem immediately apparent. (Keep looking!) Yet at the same time, we can only see God in each other – especially in those we might otherwise push away – if we look with love. And when we look with love, we participate in a deeper, divine and shared consciousness. We reach out through the soul.

So try this very specifically, next time you are on the station platform, or at a football match, or at the hospital, or in a business meeting . . . Try to see God within those you're with. You may even be able to do this right now, by looking around you. Try to see God in the face of the person serving you at the fast food restaurant, in the eyes of the kids in the classroom – even, dare I say it, in the difficult neighbour who is playing their music too loudly.

Finally, have another look in the mirror, and this time try to see God within you. Keep looking, without prejudice, with the eyes of the soul. If Mother Teresa could see God in you, then give yourself permission to see God looking back at you in the mirror. You might like to try this for a few minutes, instead of just having a quick glance. (And it is difficult, sometimes, to look for long, I admit!) Find a time when you will not be disturbed, and breathe, and smile, and keep looking for God.

Coming home to Love

There's a line from Psalm 62 that says, 'For God alone, my soul in silence waits.' I suppose for me that's what helps to distil the essence of connecting with God in a soulful way. There is an art and a craft, I believe, to waiting for God and seeking deeper communion, just as there is to sensing our soul. And it is usually best done in stillness.

Jesus had some advice on this, in fact: 'When you pray, go into your room, close the door . . .' Find somewhere you will not be interrupted. Turn your phone off. Be willing to wait a while. Make the space for God, just as you would intentionally make the space for a friend.

One very helpful way that I have found to nurture the connection is to return to my breathing once more – breathing really does seem to underlie everything

– and to relax, and to count ten breaths, or to follow the in-breaths and out-breaths to the very end . . .

But after a period of doing this, it's then a gently powerful thing to contemplate the way God *breathed* life into the dust, as we touched upon with the Genesis creation account, and in the process created a living being or soul.

I am God-breathed.

So once you have brought all your attention and awareness to your breathing, start to imagine that you are being breathed *through* – that you are not the one doing the breathing, but that God is breathing through you. Just stay with that thought, and that sense of connection to God, as you continue to be breathed. Let this transform the moment, from simply focusing on your breath, to communing deeply with God as you yield to this process. You can experience the most intimate and precious sense of God's presence within you, closer than you can ever have imagined. And it's a remarkable thing to realise this presence has been there all along.

*　　*　　*

The psalmists really were on to something, and the writer of Psalm 139 helps to remind us that it's not God who goes absent for so much of the time; it's us.

Where can I go from your Spirit?
Where can I flee from your presence?

If I go up to the heavens, you are there;
If I make my bed in the depths, you are there.

This is one of the reasons I find the techniques of mindfulness that we explored so helpful, because I am absent and distracted for so much of the time, yet when I 'show up', when I become 'present', I also become present to God, and God's presence.

And while God does not need us, I believe that God loves us. The Bible says, very simply, that 'God *is* love'. So the welcome home we can expect, and the nature of the presence we experience when we return there, is characterised by love. Love is how we recognise the presence of God.

When we come back home to Love, then, we come back to Life. And in the moments of soulful awakening we experience with – for example – a rainbow; or when we stand by a graveside; or when we listen to a sublime aria; or when we glimpse a sunrise – *here* is the reminder to keep the channel open. To come back home to Love, and Life, and to stay there. To wait, within that moment, and to be breathed into life, as part of the beauty of creation, and to remain at home within it as a living, loving part of that beauty.

To be a flesh-and-blood expression of God's love and life to the world around us, and to remember that the presence is forever there.

11

To breathe the larger air: nature and the human soul

'There is something fierce, free, and genuine that longs to find expression through your one particular and wild life.' Mary Reynolds Thompson

It's easy enough to see how we have become *disconnected* from our place in the natural world; it's so much more convenient, after all, to watch a stunning nature programme on high-definition TV than it is to put your coat on and get out into the woods to smell leaf and earth, or to stand patiently and wait, and wait, and watch for a shy bird or animal; or to climb a tree and feel a frisson of adventure, as if you were a child once more, and to let the bark get under your fingernails.

Remember when you climbed trees?

The everyday 'worlds' we inhabit today have become so increasingly artificial that they detach us from nature; and for as long as we remain wired to screens, or slaves to the 24/7 working culture, or captivated and distracted by the cathedral-like malls of consumer culture, we will grow further apart from the seasons, from the land, from the majesty of the animals and the healing properties of plants, from the way things grow, from ancient pathways, the patterns of the weather, the signs in the sky . . .

The good news, however, is that when we step out of our artificial environments and back into a more natural habitat of rivers and fields and air and trees and hills and valleys, it doesn't take long to recalibrate. We can breathe! And we can relax, too, as we really don't need to impress the egret who is patiently waiting to catch fish in the stream, or the beech trees that are coming into leaf. When we get outside, a mysteriously soulful exchange begins: for as we reconnect with forgotten or unexplored natural places, they in turn reconnect us with forgotten or unexplored places of our inner life.

*　　*　　*

I love to imagine sometimes, when I am out walking, that the outside world around me is, in fact, my inner world – as if, for instance, the river I am strolling beside, and the kingfisher that flashes past in a streak of iridescence, is a river running through me, and is a part of me that has been flowing, unnoticed, deep within. It might speak to me of an inner wisdom or imagination that I have yet fully to tap, or a sense of flow or energy that is there to draw from. And there is always more to discover: untrodden pathways, hidden gateways, forests, well-springs . . .

Everywhere I go, I find that the outside connects me to the inside, and the inside connects to the outside, if I allow it – and it is the soul that makes this deeper connection possible. So that if I were to pause by a tree for even just a few moments, and stare up into the space between the branches and leaves, then it would do my soul good, for a space opens inside of me, as I watch, which assures me that there is enough room in my life, within and without, and enough time, for what really matters.

*   *   *

Most of us have settled for a smaller-than-necessary, diminished identity, which we fashion for ourselves using the limited imagination of our ego; we draw our self-image(s) from a relentless (and poisoned) stream of adverts, and we label ourselves restrictively in terms of the roles we play or the jobs we have, and we derive our sense of worth from the praise and criticism of others alone. In the process, we have forgotten who we are. Nature helps us to remember, as the nature writer Mary

Reynolds Thompson suggests. 'The wild soul – who you really are – gets its sense of power and imagination from the natural world,' she writes, 'and thrives on an altogether different set of values: creativity, authenticity, diversity.'

Some brave people will go on wilderness retreats, staying out in the wild – in the woods, or the mountains, or the desert, for example – for nights on end in order to reconnect with their wilder soul and to loosen their grip on the smaller identity their ego has created for them. Others, meanwhile, simply feel a gorgeous sense of homecoming to nature when they go on a weekend camping trip, or indulge in some wild swimming.

Here are four ways I have found to reconnect with the natural world, and for the natural world to reconnect with us.

1. Step outside . . . and receive what comes

You never quite know what you will receive from the natural world when you step out into it. And that is part of the joy. So try to be open to whatever comes your way.

I was once leading a retreat in springtime for a group of people. The aim was to connect with some of the inspiring themes of the season, such as new life, fresh growth, green shoots . . . We planned to sit in meadows and watch butterflies and dragonflies, and let them speak to us of metamorphosis and transformation. We thought we would listen to birdsong. I could see it in my mind's eye, our group lazily enjoying a soulful treat, and soaking up the warmth of the sun and the promise of lighter, brighter days to come.

Except that, when the day itself came, it was a record low temperature for May, the wind was tormenting, and even with several layers of technical clothing on, we were shivering from the start. Not a butterfly in sight, not a dragon-fly, no bird song or early summer wonder. It's at times like that, as a retreat guide, that you wish you could control the weather.

And yet: as the day unfolded, and as we moved from wishing things were different to embracing what the unseasonal elements had to teach us, we were pushed positively to the wilder edges of soul. It's one thing to enjoy the blessings of a perfect springtime scene (a delight in its own way), but to face the imperfection and discomfort of what nature can throw at you takes you deeper into your own elemental nature. It forced us to remember that life is often uncontrollable, unpredictable, and we felt stronger and richer for having glimpsed something less tame and domesticated than we had planned for. It was soulful, but not as we expected. We learned more through this connection, and we won't forget it.

Our ego struggles to cope with unpleasant surprises, because we prefer to have things planned out, and for them to go our way; the soul, on the other hand, is so expansive that it has the capacity to welcome and receive the wilder twists and turns, and for these, in turn, to show us more of who we were created to be, beyond the boundaries of our limited imagination. It's not always easy to let the reactive commentary in the mind subside when our day doesn't go according to plan, but if we pause to breathe, and relax, and meet the 'unexpected' with a soulful embrace, we will learn, in time, that the soul will take and transform what the ego wants to reject.

Perhaps you have discovered something more about yourself through being surprised by nature.

* * *

One summer's day I was up a mountain in the French Alps, walking with my family. It was a hot August afternoon, the meadow flowers were in full bloom, and there was hardly a cloud in sight; we were in shorts and t-shirts, and had zipped up on a chair-lift for a short stroll – our three young children, two of their cousins, plus a great aunt with a bad knee! From seemingly out of nowhere, a storm cloud appeared on the horizon, and began heading our way at speed. Inexperienced in the mountains, we were woefully unprepared for it. Within minutes, the sky was darker than granite, we could feel the thunder in our chests, and worse still, we could see streaks of lightning. Before long, we weren't just under the cloud, we were in it; darkness covered us, the heavens opened, and forked lightning stabbed at the trees around us. I have never felt more scared as I cradled my one-year-old daughter under my coat. The chair-lifts were inoperable and we had no choice but to start off on foot down the mountain while the paths under our flip-flopped feet turned into fast-flowing streams of icy rainwater. We sang songs to try to keep the children calm.

Yet within all this unfolding drama, I experienced a purity of fear that I had never felt before. It wasn't that nasty, low-grade worry that accompanies the anxieties of ego – I wasn't concerned about how I looked, or what people might think of me. Instead I felt fearfully alive, as if for the first time, as I found a hidden strength and courage, and focused unswervingly on getting my family down the mountain safely. From that day on, the anxiousness of ego has never seemed quite as potent as it once did.

My soul came alive; and I discovered thunder and lightning within it.

2. Cultivate your relationship with nature

How is your relationship with the Earth? It can be abusive, one-sided and uncaring; it can be loving, intimate and soulful.

I encourage people, when we are on retreat, to use natural features of the landscape such as trees, rivers, pathways, hills, animals, birds and so forth to help them to connect more soulfully. I might suggest, for example, that they pause simply to be 'with' a well-spring, and to let their soul engage with it in a way that takes them beyond words or rational thoughts, to help them reconnect with the source of energy, wisdom, love, courage, faith or life that's there to discover within them.

It might seem strange at first to stop and just 'be' within nature; we are normally relentlessly on the go, trying to get from A to B as quickly as we can. But head outdoors without the need to go anywhere in particular, to spend time with one or two of those natural features, and you may discover a deeper sense of relationship with the natural world.

Let's take trees, for example, especially the grand old ones. They exude a depth, a presence, a resonance, that invites you to linger longer, and to enjoy the cathedral-like space that opens up within their leaves and branches. It's poignant to sit under the boughs of an old tree, because you can feel sheltered, and protected, and alive to something more. There's an oak tree not far from where I live that's been there for over a thousand years. For a millennium, it has *been* there . . . rooted, growing, shedding, and present not just to the turning of the seasons but to the centuries as well. That old tree has soul, and it touches mine.

You could try what's called a standing meditation, which is a lovely exercise: stand close to a tree like this, and imagine that you, too, have roots that reach into the soil, and branches that reach out. Imagine them growing. Spend some time reaching in to contemplate what roots *you*; and then consider how you reach out to others.

While you are there, ask yourself how you have grown over this last little while. How patient are you when it comes to the way you are growing *into* your life? When you feel like moving on (the restless mind will never want your body to stay still for very long, so make sure you notice this), stay a while longer, and practise patience. The tree, after all, has been going nowhere fast, yet it stands tall, resplendent and assured in its own skin. Can you do likewise?

* * *

You can cultivate a relationship with particular features in your own local landscape – places that are good to return to, such as a favourite tree, a hill, a clearing, a bridge, a stream. These can become soulful places for you to visit in the midst of a busy or difficult day or week. Frequently we default to the ego when we are busy; we simply forget to be present and our anxious minds carry us away into the past or future. Reconnecting with soul, by visiting a soulful place outdoors, means that you come back home to the present, and proceed with greater soulfulness into your day.

One particularly helpful way I have found to tune in more deeply to the natural environment is to extend the loving-kindness meditation to nature itself. You may think you 'love' nature, and that's a great place to start – but when we speak of 'love' in this sense, it's usually a selfish form of love: I love chocolate, I love sport, and I love nature. Instead, let's pause to consider how we can extend love and kindness to nature, for this can help to move us from 'consuming' nature to communing with it instead.

You may like to take a slow walk beside a river, for example. But don't just walk beside it; *be* with it. You may like to listen physically to its ripples and its flow, but remember that in a sense the river is a living thing, as you are a living thing – it speaks a wisdom beyond words, if you pause for long enough to listen.

As the poet Mary Oliver puts it so beautifully in 'At the River Clarion', 'Said the river I am part of holiness.'

You don't have to have access to the countryside to do this, either, of course. In the bustle of the city, you will find trees and parks; you will glimpse natural life all around you, if you pause to look. Everywhere, life is bursting out. And if you need a true reminder of the soulful connection you can make anywhere, at any time, simply go in search of a flower that is growing up through a crack in a concrete pavement. It can remind you that your own soul tenaciously calls to you through the cracks in the concrete paving of your life. It's a wonderful exercise in itself, to look for a flower in the pavement, and when you find one, to let it speak to you of both the concrete of the ego and the flower of the soul.

*   *   *

Even a passing bird can help your soul to sing.

I love how the nature poet Edward Thomas describes the song of a nightingale: 'The swift notes', he writes, 'are each as rounded and as full of liquid sweetness as a grape . . .' How delicious! Yet there's more to this for Thomas than just the beauty of the song. We are taken somewhere beyond words, and beyond ourselves, by the notes.

'It is their inhumanity that gives them their utmost fascination', he writes in *The South Country* –

> the mysterious sense which they bear to us that earth is something more than a human estate, that there are things not human yet of great honour and power in the world . . . The very first rush and the following wail [of song] empty the brain of what is merely human and leave only what is related to the height and depth of the whole world. Here we are remote from the parochialism of humanity. The bird has admitted a larger air. We breathe deeply of it and are made free citizens of eternity.

*   *   *

One day I had to chop a dying plum tree down in the garden. I had come to love that tree; every April it heralded spring with the most bountiful cloud of blossom. Even in its death, a woodpecker came to visit it daily for weeks, which I learned to watch with love; it continued to visit the tree's lonely trunk once its branches had been felled. There were many branches and much wood to remove from my narrow garden, so one

Saturday night, instead of watching TV, I got outside and lit a small fire, and once it was burning well, gathered my family around it and kept it stoked all evening. The children toasted marshmallows and we roasted a pile of chestnuts that we'd been foraging for earlier in the day. We sat under warm rugs and a cold but dazzling autumn night sky, and we enjoyed a richer, unspoken sense of reconnection. We saw each other in a different, softer light: the warm light of flame and fire, and the cooler light of moon and stars. We remembered something about ourselves and each other, though it was too good to even try to put into words. How quickly we forget again, though. How quickly we forget.

3. Tend a garden

What makes gardening so soulful? Perhaps it has to do with cultivation: the cultivation not just of the land, but of our relationship *with* the land. For gardening is surely where we get to nurture our most intimate and loving connection with Earth, and where we find soulful harmony with God's creation.

Perhaps this is why the garden designer author Julie Moir Messervy says, 'Deep within each one of us lies a garden.'

Even in the smallest plot we can find sanctuary, learning rhythms of planting and reaping, pruning and tending, watching and waiting, and then touching and tasting the fruits of our labours. It's where we can get our nails dirty with the toil of digging and weeding, and where, through a combination of manual work, creativity, fresh air and faith, we can bid our minds be still for a time, and yield instead to the satisfying ache of the body and the stirring of the soul.

Some people are blessed with a God-given touch and a fecund relationship with the soil; they can almost whisper their garden into life, coaxing fruitfulness from clods. I can't. My garden will not win awards. But still, I cherish the space it opens in my life, and I've found that even a little time spent clearing a patch of weeds, or planting seeds, or pruning the apple tree, can calm and reconnect and settle me into this present moment most palpably.

There is, of course, something positively relaxing and therapeutic about repetitive manual work, and when it is combined with the organic nature of gardening, it can bring deep restoration. (After all, who can hurry a giant pumpkin into maturity, or force a cherry tree into blossom?) The garden also provides an earthed and earthy wisdom that reminds us, as Rumi said, that 'nothing can grow unless the earth is turned over and crumbled'; or that 'unless a seed falls to the ground and dies', as Jesus said, 'it remains only a single seed, but if it dies, it bears much fruit'. We learn, in the garden, that winter is necessary, if painful; and that life is a mystery, waiting, like spring, to burst forth.

You don't have to have a garden, of course, to be a gardener. Simply growing seeds in a pot can be a soulful way of tending your relationship with creation. During Lent I have sometimes grown sweet peas from seeds as a spiritually symbolic act; over the course of forty days they tend to sprout and grow – and when they eventually flower after Easter, I don't know why I find it so moving, but it somehow gives me an added glimpse of what growth and colour and life looks like.

Whenever you get your hands dirty in a garden, the very act itself places you necessarily into the rhythms and cycles of the seasons. For you cannot do anything meaningfully as a gardener without knowing where you are within the cycle of the year. As such, gardening is a sacred act; it's as if we are being planted back in creation, even as we plant; and we find ourselves growing, even as we watch and wait for the garden to grow.

4. Witness the seasons

The rhythm of the seasons speaks deeply to us and connects us at a profound level with the universe and its own rhythms and cycles and seasons. As well as getting into the garden, there are many ways to step back into the rhythm of the seasons.

I will explore how to engage soulfully with both autumn and winter in Part 4, through welcoming the paradoxical nature of autumn (its melancholy and its fruitfulness), and embracing the darkness of winter with a cosiness of the soul that the Danes call *hygge*.

But one specific and simple way to notice where you are with the seasons and the cycles of the created world is to mark the solstices and the equinoxes. So with *winter*, you could mark the shortest day – the solstice

– by going for a walk while it is light, for example, and watching the sun set, and returning home in the dark. That day of greatest gloom is a turning point, of course, as the Earth tilts once more towards the light of the sun, and the days start to get longer. You don't necessarily need to do more than notice it and get out into the day – although you could, of course, journal the experience as an intentional way of 'finding yourself' there, in the heart of winter darkness.

Marking the equinox in *spring* is likewise a helpful milestone in the year. It's a moment of equal daylight and darkness, but a time when the light is advancing. During spring, you may wish to reflect upon new ways you've begun to grow; or to be thankful for signs of life where previously the ground of your being seemed dormant. Look for those signs of life around you – contemplate leaf buds, daffodils or bluebells, and let them encourage you that warmth is on its way!

Summer brings its more obvious blessings of lighter and lazier days. And once again, there is a solstice that marks (this time) the longest day, on which I love to rise to greet the dawn. To go out and sit on a hill and wait and watch for the first light is a soulful and moving act of reconnection with the rhythms of the solar system. Summer is, of course, a time for holidays, and for pausing for breath within the busyness of the year; it gives us a chance to regain perspective (if indeed we take a proper break, and manage to disconnect from work e-mails, for instance, when we are away!).

I remember one year when I had a slightly longer holiday than usual. In the first few days, I felt the stress and strain of my busy schedule coursing through me. It takes time to let it go. I began to relax during the middle days of my time away. And then, by the very end of my break, I discovered a profound thing (which I wouldn't normally have done, except that I had a few extra days to enjoy): I was now able to sit and watch the clouds move slowly by, from my balcony, and savour the painfully – yet pleasurably – slow progress of the scene unfolding before me.

When I returned home and re-entered the fray of normal life, I looked back upon my cloud-watching with slight embarrassment – could I have done something more useful with my time? I didn't even read! So imagine my delight when I discovered a TED talk by Gavin Pretor-Pinney, who founded the Cloud Appreciation Society. Watching clouds, he says, gives us an excuse to do something we almost never allow ourselves to do: *nothing*. But it also reconnects us profoundly with creation. 'We are creatures which inhabit this ocean of air,' he says. 'We don't just live beneath the sky – we live within it.' Summer is the perfect time for remembering this, and for finding rest for the soul. If you do nothing but watch the clouds for an afternoon, you have acted purposefully and wisely and with soul.

Autumn is perhaps the most vivid of seasons, both for its wondrous displays of colourful leaves and yet the melancholy that accompanies their falling. As Brian

McLaren puts it so well, 'For all its angst, there's beauty in perplexity, the autumn blaze of colour between green and gone.'

If you're like me, you'll experience a bass-note sense of sadness during autumn, which heralds both the end of summer (always sad!) and a gentle reminder that the leaves of our life must fall, and that we all face our own autumn and winter in the end.

Yet autumn yields a fruitfulness, and a 'ripenening to the core', as Keats puts it so evocatively in his wonderful ode 'To Autumn', which is to be savoured and celebrated, too. You may not feel that your life is outwardly successful, especially in the eyes of the world, yet fruitfulness is not measured by bank balances or job titles . . .

Autumn is also a time for the most abundant scattering of seeds. Life here will go on, in the end, without us. Yet our life's work will have scattered and planted seeds in many places, even without our knowing; seeds that may take root and grow strong way beyond our lifetimes. How could we enjoy the shelter and shade of a mighty oak, after all, had it not begun, centuries before, by falling to the ground as a tiny acorn?

We reach out through soul . . . with love

Soul connects us, interweaves us, then, with God, with each other, with place, and with nature and the seasons. In those times of connection, it can provide us with 'hints of congruence', as the theologian Eugene Peterson puts it, 'between who and what we are, and the world around us – rocks and trees, meadows and mountains, birds and fish, dogs and cats, kingfishers and dragon-flies ... obscure and fleeting, but convincing confirmations that we are all in this together, that we are kin to all that is and all that will be'.

And this is crucial: for soul repositions us; it stops us being spectators, and reminds us that we are in relationship with all things. And when we reach out through soul, we can only reach out with love. It is the characteristic of soul *par excellence*. We touched earlier upon three hallmarks of the ego, which involve competing, controlling and endlessly comparing ourselves with others. That's how to recognise when the ego is driving us, and when we're reacting mindlessly. Well, the hallmark of soul is love, and it draws us towards loving reconnection with all parts of life.

What does love look like? Paul described it as this, in the passage from the Bible that is so often quoted at weddings. Try to read it with fresh eyes, and pause upon each phrase, to let it speak again.

Love is patient, love is kind. It does not envy, it does not boast. It does not dishonour others, it is not self-seeking, it is not easily angered, it keeps no record of wrongs. Love does not delight in evil but rejoices with the truth. It always protects, always trusts, always hopes, always perseveres.

This kind of love is possible within all our relationships, not just the human ones.

A word of warning, however, before we begin to feel too fuzzy and warm. Love comes with a cost. Paul's description of love is beautiful, but it is also utterly challenging. If we are, indeed, 'all in this together' – and if, through soulful reconnection with God, each other and nature in particular we begin to shift from consuming the world to communing with it instead, then we simply cannot continue as before. Soulfulness is not about a nice walk in the country to feel better about ourselves. It is about reaching out and reconnecting, but this time in love. This requires that we wake up from our sleep, that we become mindful of the way our lifestyles are *abusing* the relationship we have with each other, God and the planet, and that we ask how we can proceed soulfully, with greater love for all. Today.

12

The space between us

To conclude Part 3, in which we have considered reaching out through soul, in love, to the world around us, I'd like us to contemplate the role of place and space in our reaching out.

There's a little church that's no bigger than a room, really, over an archway close to where I live. And on an autumn afternoon, if the sun is out, the light streams through its simple windows to create a uniquely touching place in which to sit and pause for a while; in which to do nothing much but practise the often challenging art of being. It's what we might call 'good for the soul' in there; it is enlivening, restorative, inspiring.

But how does a room *do* that? And what makes me, and so many other passers-by, want to return to that soulful space again and again, to soak up its energy? It has that same quality of soulfulness, which whispers of more; and when you step into its literal space, it's as if you're stepping into a different kind of world. A world that's been hidden in plain sight, all along, within the screaming, shouting, shiny world of ego.

*　　*　　*

Some places such as this church are very still – inanimate, almost – and their very stillness is part of their appeal. But other soulful places brim over with life, like the best kind of cafés. Most of us have a favourite haunt at which, almost intuitively, we just love to hang out. Most likely, it's not a 'chain' or a franchise; it's probably somewhere small and independent, tucked away down a side street, off the beaten track. It might be somewhere individual, artistic or idiosyncratic. Perhaps the combination of the decor and the music is what does it for you, whatever 'it' is; or the loving care and attention that the barista pours into their coffee-making. It could just be the atmosphere, which is shaped through a combination of people and presences. But whatever it is, this is a *good* place to be, and once again, it's a place you'll keep returning to.

*　　*　　*

In his ever-fascinating weekend column for the *Observer* newspaper, the psychologist Oliver Burkeman once asked: What makes a *place* soulful? And why do 'non-religious people' (like him) feel 'the spine shiver of something ... transcendent, divine' when they visit what the Celts called thin places? (Thin places are the kind of landscapes where the veil between heaven and Earth seems thinner. They are often threshold places, such as mountains [where the land meets the sky] or shorelines [where sea meets land]; but they can be any place that connects or inspires you.)

There are rational attempts to explain the pull of such places – we feel the emotional residue of previous visitors, perhaps, or there's a stronger electro-magnetic field ... But Burkeman concludes: 'We're in the territory of the ineffable ... Explanations aren't merely useless; they threaten to get in the way. The experience of a thin place feels special because words fail, leaving stunned silence.'

He's right; a place, in its own assured stillness, can cut straight through a restless mind (which wants to capture, explain or distil the experience) to connect with our soul instead. At which point we can sense that deeper joy of being still within stillness, being beautiful within beauty, being blessed within blessing. Ineffably so.

* * *

So imagine if we could bring something more of the soulfulness of those times back with us, into the day to day, to help to change the quality and nature of the world around us. To create the kind of soul space around us in which we can stretch, grow and flourish. And, crucially, to open up the kind of soul space around us that others can step into, to be inspired, and energised, and reconnected. This might be through specific physical spaces we create; it may also be simply through our own soulful presence.

Creating intentional soul space around us

Each month on a Friday night, a small group of us gather around a kitchen table, and we light a candle or two, eat some home-baked bread, drink some wine, and share how it's been going. We might ponder a few lines of poetry, too, or look at a piece of art together; sometimes we say a prayer or simply sit in a dignified and intentional silence. It's what I would describe as a 'soulful' space, and personally, in the warp and weft of twenty-first-century Western culture, it's a space I need to enter, as it brings me back to life. This is an example of some intentional space that you can create in order to help you, and others, to give your soul space to breathe and stretch and feed!

The power of soulful presence

But then you can also create space around you through your very presence. Some people have an anxious presence and they need to fill the space around them with talk and with ego. This stifles the space for their – or your – soul to 'be'. Perhaps you can think of someone with whom you almost feel claustrophobic in their presence, because it's filled with talk, filled with ego, filled with posing, filled with insecurity.

Stepping into the presence of someone with soul, however, can be like stepping into a beautiful café or an art gallery or a sanctuary. Your soul stirs, because it is inspired to do so, and has the room to do so. Your soul stirs because the soul is present in the soulful woman or man you are with. And your souls are able to meet within the soulful space between you.

I wonder what kind of space you love to step into. You might like to reflect on this now. Perhaps you have a particular room, or café, or gallery space, or outdoor place, or church, or cathedral, where you go in order to give your soul room to breathe, and where you feel somehow calmed but energised, inspired, reset, uplifted, renewed . . .

Now, consider the kind of space you create around you. You could think first about the physical space – what your home is like, or your room, or your office or place of work. You might even have a shed in the garden or some form of 'sanctuary' to which you can retreat. What is the nature of the space around you? What can you do to clear some space within the space, so that it's not too cluttered or busy? What have you placed within the space to inspire you (pictures, furniture, books, favourite items and so on)? How does the space help to reconnect you?

Recently, I went to buy a bookcase for my little writing hut at the end of the garden. The hut provides a space in which to work, but it's also one in which I try to practise stillness and silence – so I wanted the furniture to fit not only the dimensions but also the 'feel'. We have a shop along the road that sells reclaimed pieces of furniture, and they had some items that I thought could work. I was drawn to one in particular that, while it wasn't perfect, had a certain soulful quality about it . . . When I got the bookcase back to the hut, it felt as if it had always belonged here. The way the sun fell upon it, the way the books sat within it, the way it was; it felt right. And fascinatingly, this simple object now manages to connect me to this space, here, in a more inspiring way. The space comes more fully alive. Perhaps it carries something of the soulfulness of the man or woman who crafted it in the first place. Perhaps it was simply that they crafted it with love. But that simple piece of furniture helps, now, to make the space what it is.

Creating space through your presence

When someone steps into your presence, how, I wonder, can you help them to feel that sense of calmed but inspired connection that you get from stepping into your own favourite space? What would it take to nurture that kind of presence wherever you go, staying mindful to the possibility of opening up soul space within even some of the most cramped and suffocating personal situations? Imagine if the next person you met experienced a 'spine shiver of something . . .

transcendent' merely by stepping into the space of your presence.

You can enter 'space' yourself simply by engaging with one or two of our mindful exercises, wherever you find yourself. It never ceases to amaze me how much space seems to open up within you when you stop to remember your breathing, and to pause, and to be still for a moment. You can move from feeling as if everything were crowding you out, to becoming aware of the space within and around you. Within those busiest moments, remember to count your ten breaths, for example, and *enter* the space.

The depth and assurance that accompanies those rare people with truly soulful presence comes from their having reached in, to experience more of their own soulful self, before then reaching out, in love, to the world around them. But there is a spacious quality about them, which arises from their unhurried nature, their being fully attentive, their being tuned in and present to what's before them – and it's enviable. This is not, however, an unattainable state of spiritual Zen-like being they've found. It is a soulful, loving presence that we all have about us, if we allow it the space to make its presence felt.

*　　　*　　　*

Parker Palmer, who writes very powerfully about the soul, argues that the ego builds a wall around the soul, and the person you usually connect with is the insecure imposter who is play-acting 'front of house'. The soul is there, but out of sight.

When we are in company, if we stay positively anchored to the soul, instead of play-acting from front of house, we are able to maintain a certain quality of assured solitude (instead of reactive neediness) which opens up space for those around us to connect with us. Likewise, when we are alone, we are able to rest in the assurance that we are powerfully connected through the soul, to others, to God, to the world around us. We do not need to be with them in order to know we are part of them and they are a part of us. Thus, whether we are in company or alone, we can reach in for soul, and reach out through soul, and we meet lovingly in that space between us.

Part 4
Living with soul: giving flesh-and-blood expression to the soulful life

13

Fleshing out our unique, inner aliveness

Soul is not a disembodied, floaty state of esoteric escapism. Quite the contrary; it is fleshed out – full-blooded and full-bodied, like a glass of vintage wine. This may not seem like the most 'spiritual' way of seeing things, because so often, as we have touched upon in Part 2, we mistakenly believe that spirituality must offer us an escape from the so-called material realm and usher us into the world of pure spirit instead. This is where we must beware of disappearing into a movement such as mindfulness purely for the sake of escaping our worries or troubles, or for the sake of becoming ultra-spiritual in a way that denies the physicality of life.

Another principle that I find crucially distinctive within the Judaeo-Christian tradition, then, is *incarnation*, which compels me to believe that the real journey in life involves travelling fully back into, not away from, the flesh-and-blood reality of our existence. It is a loving reconnection with, or embrace of, life.

Judaism has always been deeply rooted, earthed as it were, in the day to day; it celebrates eating and drinking (as well as fasting!), festivity, seasons and cycles, and it finds the sacred well and truly embedded in the ordinary, like letters running through a stick of rock.

Meanwhile Christianity, which flows out of Judaism, centres on 'the Word made flesh'; on God becoming human, in Jesus. This is what Christmas is about, as Christians celebrate 'the incarnation' and remember, in the words of the poet Christina Rossetti, the time that 'Love came down'. Note the trajectory here: the spiritual principle is that God shows us not the way out of this world, but a way to be more wholly within it.

It's a way back in, which seeks to embrace and transform through love.

The notion of God becoming human – recorded so poetically and evocatively in the prologue to John's Gospel – may feel too 'cosmic' for our small minds to grasp, but we can, nevertheless, draw energy and inspiration from the principle. The most practical response we can make is to turn and head back *into* the world from which we might otherwise and hitherto have been seeking to escape, to be part of the goodness that helps to transform it.

* * *

With incarnation, the invisible is made manifest. We *embody* something hitherto unseen, which is of true worth and beauty.

Branding experts talk about this a lot; if you 'live your values', they say, you'll establish and maintain the authenticity of your brand. It's one thing to subscribe to a value such as 'Show you care', for example, and to post it on your website; it's another thing to demonstrate it through the way you treat not just your customers but your suppliers and your employees.

Now, soulfulness is not about maintaining the authenticity of a brand; but incarnation *is* certainly about embodying what we hold most dear and who we most truly are. It's about giving expression to our unique, inner aliveness, fleshing this out, making it visible through acts of love.

Consider for a few moments how you embody the soulful qualities that you reflected upon above using the eight derivations of the word *nephesh* (a living being, life, self, a person, desire, passion, appetite and emotion). What is it that you love and live for, and how would the people who know you best describe what this looks like in your life? What do you hunger and thirst for, and how is this expressed through your actions? How does life itself find authentic expression through what you do?

And what might you like to do, in order to bring more of this soulfulness to expression through your life? What changes could you make? If you were to do one thing differently today, in order to live more fully as an expression of your soulful self, what could you do?

* * *

If we can indeed turn around and face back into our present reality, we can start to bring life to the ordinary, and the ordinary to life. Day in, day out. For incarnation also implies that the *whole* of our life matters, and that the smallest and seemingly most insignificant parts of it are just as important as some of the greatest. If we consider this in terms of the life of our community, too, then we must also remember that every person matters, however seemingly insignificant. In fact, they give us a window onto the most significant: the principle of 'the last will be first, and the first will be last', as spoken by Jesus, challenges to the core our automatic assumptions about what or who matters most in life.

We could even argue that the way we attend to the smaller things sets the tone and affects the very nature and scope of the rest of our life. How we drink our tea, or do the washing-up, as we considered earlier; how we greet the person at the front desk of the office; how we get the children out of the door to school ... These are not tasks to get out of, or just to get through, but to get *in* to. For with incarnation, the way *through* is the way *in*.

Get into it!

Each morning when I sit down to write I am faced with a blank page, and I can feel anxious to fill it. The temptation is either to procrastinate (to get out of it) or to rush on quickly (to get through it). If I do either, then I miss both the joy *and* the pain of the process itself. And the journey matters – how we get there helps to determine where we end up, after all. Needless to say, how present I am to the craft of writing, in this case, *will* affect the quality of the words, just as it will affect the quality of whatever you turn your hand to next. 'Getting *in* to' it will – in the end – carry us through, but in a deeper way, at a better pace. With love. It's not always easy, but no one promised that it should be.

* * *

I notice myself trying to get *through* life all the time. Recently, I set about painting a wooden cabinet that we'd bought from a second-hand shop. It was a chance to do some up-cycling, as they call it. We bought some lovely paint, and I set about the task. Minutes in, I noticed I was tense, and rushing, and (once again) merely trying to get the job done as quickly as I could. So I took a few deep breaths, settled back into my soul, and settled in to the process itself. The 'task' was transformed: no longer did this feel like a job to tick off, but a way of becoming soulfully present to a simple act of re-creation.

And here is one secret, I believe: I focused on bringing not just care and attention to the process, but also love. I'm no master-craftsman, sadly, but I tried to imagine and to embody the kind of love that a master-craftsman might bring to their work. And so the task of painting itself became an expression for me of something more: it slowed me down, helped me to become present, and allowed me to create something that I can now take delight in.

When we participate in the act of creating, or re-creating, we step away from the deadening consumerist mindset that objectifies the material world and makes it disposable, and instead we develop a relationship with what's around us, and participate actively in the aesthetics of our daily life, however simple those aesthetics may be. That's surely why the world of up-cycling, of reusing and reclaiming and reimagining old or unwanted objects, has provided a soulful antidote to life in a rampantly consumerist and disposable world. We slow down, we relate, we become present, we create, we give expression to something that otherwise would have had none, we love.

14

Hygge – a warm and soulful embrace of the whole of life

Incarnation helps us to start where we are. So often, we are tempted to believe that life will really begin in earnest when our circumstances change, or when we reach some imagined point in the future, or when we become well again, for instance. This can mean that we are always seeking to escape from here in order to get to *there*. Incarnation transports us, if you like, fully back into the present, which is the only place in which change can ever happen.

As Jon Kabat-Zinn puts it so powerfully, 'There is no successful escaping from yourself in the long run, only transformation.'

This extends to the whole of life, not just to the extremes or to life-threatening addictions. I can try all I like to escape my humdrum evenings or the stress of a long, busy day by watching more TV while I surf the social media on my smart-phone, and there is comfort in the forgetting and distraction. But when it's our escape route, there's nothing transformational about it. TV, Internet, religion, shopping, alcohol, drugs, work . . . they can all be used as quick ways out if we are not careful. We can easily develop a mentality that defaults to escape, especially within a contemporary culture that is stressful and often overbearing and sells escape back to us at an inflated price.

The soulful way, however, is not to escape, but to confront our reality, and to lovingly reconnect with it, which helps transform it. Something good can emerge from within even the darkest or most difficult circumstances when we resist the urge to flee and instead we reach to embrace.

* * *

With that in mind, I love the principle of *hygge* (pronounced *hyerga*), which is the Danish way of tackling some of the coldest and darkest winters you can experience in the northern hemisphere. *Hygge* is not a form of escape, but a way of living *within* the difficult conditions, which in turns helps to transform them into something beautiful – while providing great inspiration for us all, wherever we find ourselves. The Danes, lest we forget, are officially some of the happiest people on the planet (according to the annual World Happiness Report), and *hygge* is part of the reason why.

Hygge, then, is a concept, an idea, a way of being – hard to define precisely, and even harder to translate, but it relates to a state of cosy yet profound simplicity. It is about the lovely, simple pleasures of life – such as drawing the curtains against the dark and the cold, lighting candles, kindling a fire, putting on your warm socks, making a hot drink and settling in with a group of friends or relatives.

But it's as much about the philosophy behind it, too, which celebrates being together with others, giving and receiving, making deeper connections, feeling more rooted, creating a calm and beautiful atmosphere in which to rest, and ultimately being present, with no agenda beyond the *hygge* itself.

The Danish anthropologist Jeppe Trolle Linnet suggests that Danes have a different set of priorities to many of us fellow Westerners who are very achievement oriented, and who end up struggling as a result. While the Danes feel 'uncomfortable talking about their accomplishments and ambitions', he says, 'the highest honor that you can claim is that you are happy and that you are really content with the way you have lived'. *The highest honour that you can claim is that you are happy!* What a breath of fresh air, compared with the way so many of us prattle on about how busy or stressed we are.

Hygge is 'good for the soul', suggests Helen Russell, author of *The Year of Living Danishly: Uncovering the Secrets of the World's Happiest Country*. 'There isn't so much enforced deprivation in Denmark,' she says. 'Instead you're kinder to yourselves and so each other. Danes don't binge then purge . . .'

Hygge is therefore not the escape *from*, but the diving deeper into. There will always be things we don't like about life, whether it's the weather, or how we look, or the way our boss is managing us. Soulfulness is learning to be – like the Danes – fully within our situation, to bring warmth and goodness to bear, even as the cold bites.

So be proactive. Why not convene an evening for some of your close friends or family, when you can brew some coffee, eat some simple home-cooked food, make a fire, light candles, perhaps read some poetry or play your favourite songs to each other, or even sing some songs! – and create for yourselves a soulful space in which you can help to transform the nature and quality of your evening, by being within it instead of trying to escape from it. You could also try something slightly more daring, which is to sit in quietness together for a while, and just watch the candles dance.

Here, again, we remember how soulfulness is very much rooted in the physical – from a pair of warm, cosy socks to flickering candles or freshly baked bread – yet it connects us to something more. Throw in a piece of inspiring art or poetry and it is almost as if we are transported somewhere else – but the joy is that we are not: instead we have become more fully here, and 'where we are' has become a more soulful space, a place now with deeply transformational qualities to it.

* * *

Sometimes, it's not so much about cosiness as intentional acceptance of a situation, but in a way that is kind to yourself and that honours the place you find yourself in. A friend of mine felt sad that his wife, a newly qualified paramedic, was scheduled to work on Christmas Eve evening and into Christmas Day. He loves Christmas Eve, it's his favourite day of the year, and he knew that it would not be the same without her. What he resolved to do, however, was – instead of 'wishing' his situation were different (and when does wishing get us anywhere?) – to sit quietly and intentionally, and to honour her absence, and to witness his own sadness, and to embrace the reality of that small but not insignificant loss.

There is a form of prayer that I find very helpful in this regard, called 'welcoming prayer', in which you sit quietly and pay attention to the emotions you are feeling, and instead of pushing them away, welcome them. (That's not to say you have to welcome what's caused sadness, for instance, but you can welcome the feelings that arise. There is room within you for them.) In this way, you are present to them, not trying to escape from them. The final part of the prayer is, if you so wish, to hand your feelings to God, and to ask God to help you with them. It's not seeking spiritual escape, but a soulful embrace of 'where you are'. If we recall the wonderful idea that God is *anam cara*, then we can sit with our situation courageously, and ask to experience more of a sense of God's help, friendship and presence within the moment. Light a candle, too, or use something symbolically significant to you, such as a photograph or keepsake, which can help you to settle into the moment. Open up the kind of soul space we touched upon earlier, in which your own soul may breathe, and through which you may meet this moment in a loving and soulful way.

*　　*　　*

At one of the gatherings around our kitchen table I mentioned at the end of Part 3, one of our number invited her friend for the evening (she'd been staying for a day or two). This lady had not experienced this kind of thing before, where a group of people gather intentionally to be together, and to share stories, and to light candles, and to 'be'. We invited her (as we do with most guests) to share something of her story with us. Who was she? Where did she come from? What could she tell us about what had brought her to this point in time? She felt a bit embarrassed (the ego in most of us would pipe up if we were put on the spot: 'Who – me? I don't have anything interesting to share . . .'), but I'm glad to say she shared, and we listened quite well, at the soulful level, and didn't fall into too many of Russ Parker's pitfalls. After she had spoken, we asked her some follow-up questions, and at the end of it our guest began to cry. Not tears of sadness, but of release and perhaps even joy. She explained, quite simply, that no one had ever invited her to share her story in that way before, let alone actually *listened*.

The space that we open up can be positively transformative if we create it with loving care. To listen without ego or interruption provides others with safe enough space for them to be their own self; it opens up space for the soul to surface and breathe and to make connection; and good things inevitably happen when we make that kind of space available.

The power of the hug

While there is no clear link that helps us to translate '*hygge*' into English, etymologists believe that the word shares roots with our own word 'hug', and that's a helpful connection. For it reminds us that a soulful approach to life means a warm sense of embrace. The embrace is a dynamic engagement with our situation, with the world around us and with life; it connects us, it draws us close, it is welcoming and it is loving.

It's amazing what difference a hug can make. Cast your mind back to the last time someone gave you a hug when you really needed one. What did that do for you? How did it make you feel?

There is plenty of scientific evidence to suggest that hugs affect our sense of well-being positively. People who were hugged and cuddled as babies and children display fewer stress symptoms as adults; stress is reduced by even brief touches between adults; and we are, as the psychologist Andrea Polard states, 'simply wired to find touch reassuring'. The heart rate lowers, along with the amount of the stress hormone cortisol in our system, improving our health. 'Reach out and hug, and your life might not only feel better, but last longer,' she writes. Crucially, we release the hormone oxytocin when touched, which increases our sense of attachment, connection, trust and intimacy. It may sound obvious, but 'When we're hugged, we feel less lonely.'

Paul Zak concurs. He's a 'neuro-economist' (someone who researches the relationship between economic behaviour and the brain) who presented an intriguing TED talk entitled 'Trust, Morality – and Oxytocin?'. Speaking about what he calls the 'moral molecule', he says: 'We have found that people who release oxytocin are happier, and they are happier because they have better relationships of all types.' The best and easiest way to release oxytocin is, he confirms, through hugging. Eight a day is the prescribed amount!

When we embrace life, life embraces us

Fascinatingly, according to Zak, the molecule is also released in the brain and the bloodstream through prayer – which we might reframe in our mind, for a moment, as a form of spiritual embrace. For prayer does not need to be pious, even though we tend to think of it as such; instead, it can be the equivalent of a loving embrace with those you are praying for, or, quite simply, with God.

And this, in a sense, takes us soulfully into a more relational dynamic than meditation might. The moving story of the Prodigal Son that Jesus told comes to mind – of the young man who wants to receive his inheritance while his father is still alive, and who leaves home to blow it all on fast living, loses everything, and realises it would be better to be a servant for his dad than to die of starvation. So he returns home to ask if he can work for him. As the account in Luke's Gospel puts it: 'But while he was still a long way off, his father saw him and was filled with compassion for him; he ran to his son, threw his arms around him and kissed him'.

While we often, quite naturally, see prayer as a form of request, it's so much more, because it nurtures our relationship with God. It's really an opportunity to return, daily, to the loving embrace of the Father in this story. To embrace, and to be embraced, as if we were a long-lost child. In oxytocin terms alone, it's to receive the equivalent of a physical hug, and its resulting sense of attachment, connection, trust and intimacy . . . but beyond that, it's also to deepen our embrace with life itself.

This embrace, whether physical or metaphorical, helps us to work lovingly with what we have: to bring life to our situation, and in turn to bring our situation to life. It doesn't have to be a fearful process, either; just as the Danes do within their winters, we can seek to transform our experience creatively, assuredly and beautifully, by embracing it – and by receiving *its* embrace in return.

The way to get 'into' it is to give yourself *to* it

The embrace helps to symbolise a very soulful principle – which is to give yourself to the day, to the people you meet in it, to the work you do during it . . . instead of asking what you can get out of it. By stepping into the day with an attitude of embrace, and looking to give ourselves to it, we turn the consumerist mindset on its head, and open up greater possibilities as we go.

I like to remind people who are coming on retreat with me about this. If you take a precious day out of your schedule for a retreat (especially if you are busy, and you feel guilty because you really 'should' be working!), you can end up feeling anxious about what you will get out of the process. Will it be worth the sacrifice of my time? What will I return with? Will I receive the answer I have been longing to discover? These kinds of questions can end up leaving us more attached to outcomes than might otherwise be helpful or healthy, and cause us to feel tense and less open than we otherwise might have been.

When we loosen our grip on outcomes, we can approach our day – and our life, too – with fewer expectations, yet with a greater degree of expectancy.

And by asking, 'How can I give myself most fully to this day?' the focus changes; things turn, from being transactional (what can I get?) to being *relational*. I'm not using the day, or the process, for my own benefit, in quite the same way that I might even use a mindfulness tool or technique to de-stress or to calm me down. Instead, if I seek to bring my whole being, my *nephesh*, and to be ready to offer it, in humility, to whatever lies before me in the moment – to the situation, to the people, to the work, to God – then I'm able to make a soulful connection: an embrace, shall we say. The reward, in part at least, is to discover more of the nature of my soulful self, even as I offer it up. How does offering myself to this day bless it, and the people, and the spaces, within it?

The fact that this is more about embrace than any spiritually 'correct' formula for achieving enlightenment or doing things the right way means that we can also be freed from any fear of getting it wrong. Jesus' contemporaries, listening to his story of the Prodigal Son, would have understood that the father made a cultural embarrassment of himself simply by *running* towards his son, let alone by forgiving and embracing him. There was nothing pious or religious about his act: it was socially and culturally scandalous, in fact, but it was also an arms-wide-open gesture of exuberant loving-kindness, which turned a toxic situation around and brought love back to life.

When you embrace a friend who is upset, or when you throw your arms around someone who has wronged you, you are reaching beyond any social or even spiritual barriers to a place of soul. A place beyond doctrine, a place beyond expectations, a place beyond words . . .

Recently, our daughter Mercy, who is ten, was starting to feel socially awkward and began worrying about what her friends thought of her. (Of course, she was really worrying about a fiction – about what she *thought* her friends thought of her.) She was concerned, in particular, about what they would think of what she was wearing.

My wife gently and wisely reminded her of the day, not so long ago, when she had a party – a day on which she'd also been worrying about what to wear. Most of the girls had arrived on time to the party, and everyone, of course, looked lovely. But one of her friends came late. And when this girl entered the back garden (the party was outside) and saw Mercy, she ran screaming the length of the garden, arms wide open, and hugged her for what seemed like forever, in great joy and excitement. She hadn't paused for a second to assess what Mercy was wearing. The embrace cut through any trace of ego in an instant, as this girl not only gave herself to the moment, to the party and most assuredly to my daughter, but threw herself into the whole thing with all her heart. It was a truly wonderful moment of abandon to behold.

15

Peace, wholeness and embracing paradox

The loving embrace helps us, I believe, to make peace with our situation. And peace is a significant word in our pursuit of a soulful life – for it invites us to imagine what life beyond the constant battles of ego might look like, if it's not merely the absence of noise, but the presence of something richer.

Once I was doing some retreat work with a man who had been very busy; he was working painfully hard, just like his wife, who also had a 'big' job. He hadn't seen his children as much as he would have liked, because his work was taking him away a lot; he was pushing hard, he said, because he wanted to secure a better future for his family, which is, of course, an entirely admirable and worthy motivation. But in a sense, his life had begun to feel like a battle.

It made me wonder about the nature of the 'peace' *he* was fighting for. If he could secure that future for his family, what would it look like, and how would he know when to stop battling on? For if peace, as we noted at the start of this book, is not just the absence of war – or, in our own lives, the absence of stress, overwork, over-commitment and the like – but the presence of something positive beyond that, then what kind of peace could he – and can we – hope to enter?

It's a tough question for any of us; in a sense, it's easier to keep going, to keep fighting, because it can be hard to know what to do with ourselves when the busy-ness stops. It's one thing to do a day's retreat here or there, or practise mindfulness when we remember to in order to give ourselves a break from the madness of the front line before returning to it. But how can we enter an active sense of lasting peace that's about far more than taking a few minutes out to calm down in the heat of a stressful day?

Being *at* peace

I think the Hebrew word for peace, *shalom*, points us in a helpful direction. Like many Hebrew words, it evokes far more than one strict and particular definition, offering a sense of feeling, intent and emotion, all wrapped into one. With *shalom*, then, it's well known as a form of both greeting and farewell, meaning 'Peace be with you!'; yet its sense of 'peace' carries with it a deeper evocation too, of harmony, well-being, flourishing and wholeness – all of which help us to envisage a richer way of entering peace itself. You could ask yourself about each of those categories in turn:

What kind of harmony – or discord – do the various melodies in my life create?
What does it mean to be well, and how well am I?
When I'm truly flourishing, what does that look like?

But it's the aspect of wholeness in particular that I'd like us to pause to notice here, as I believe this really helps us to be *at* peace ... with ourselves, with the world, with each other, with God.

It matters how we understand wholeness, because frequently we misconstrue it, which leads to a distinct lack of peace in our hearts. Close your eyes and think of wholeness, and you might imagine some just-out-of-reach state of perfection; like an advert for a spa, wholeness can feel like a beautiful idea, but one that is almost too good to be true. So we might embark on serial self-help courses or spirituality programmes to improve ourselves, to try to become, somehow, *better*, and thus to improve our life; yet so often we give up, because it feels as if we'll never find that place where we are 'sorted'.

The liberating news, however, is that our problems will *never* fully disappear in this life, and that wholeness was never meant to be about becoming wholly happy, wholly fulfilled or wholly sorted. We never will. So we can relax. Instead, wholeness offers us the challenge and opportunity to live deeper within the creative tension that comes with the *whole* of life; within what we perceive to be the 'bad' as well as the 'good'; within the difficult as well as the easy. Instead of trying to banish or escape from the tougher situations we face, therefore, or to find easy or neat resolution within the messiness, it's possible to be at greater peace with the wholeness of life, and with our own life, warts and all.

At peace within paradox

This may feel or sound paradoxical, because we tend to think all the time in terms of binary opposites – about things we like and don't like. We push away things that we don't like, while we pull towards us what we do. And our mind creates opposing categories to make this easier: light and dark, good and bad, us and them, pleasure and pain, health and sickness, and so on. It simplifies the way we see the world. Yet the celebrated educationist and Quaker author Parker J. Palmer highlights very helpfully the *positive* and healthy nature of paradox. 'In a paradox,' he writes, 'opposites do not negate each other – they cohere in mysterious unity at the heart of reality . . .'

Palmer uses autumn as an evocative (and soulful) example of finding peace within paradox. It's a season of beauty, he explains, but also of decay. We like the vivid display of colourful leaves but we fear the sense of loss that piles up with each one that falls. We like the fruitfulness of berries and ripe apples but we fear the mulch of mud and leaves underfoot that reminds us of where we must physically return to in the end. The themes of autumn resonate with us in a visceral way – and ultimately they speak to us, year after year, of the cycle of life and death. We like the idea of life, and we do not like the idea of death. No wonder, then, that we have mixed feelings about autumn!

Yet as Palmer puts it, 'If I try to "make" a life that defies the diminishments of autumn, the life I end with will be artificial at best, and utterly colourless as well. But when I yield to the endless interplay of living and dying, dying and living, the life I am given will be real and colourful, fruitful and whole.'

Real and colourful, fruitful and whole. This is highly significant for us on the soulful journey, as we are *not* aiming for some kind of false state of spiritual perfection, where nothing is wrong and all is OK, and everything that we consider nasty, broken or unhelpful has been swept beneath the carpet. Instead, we step into the wholeness of a peace that has colour, vibrancy, fruit . . . precisely *because* it contains loss as well as gain, death as well as life, decay as well as beauty, darkness as well as light. These are *all* parts of the mysterious whole, which cohere creatively at the heart of reality. As the Trappist monk Thomas Merton put it, 'There is in all visible things . . . a hidden wholeness.'

* * *

We often talk about finding balance in life, but I'm not convinced it's necessarily a very helpful word, for balance hints to me of inertia. Soulful characters may not always have the balance of their life right, but they do have that hidden wholeness. And they certainly have that sense of the real, the colourful, the fruitful and the whole. They might make mistakes, or go overboard, or struggle, and they are by no means perfect.

Think of someone ultra-spiritual, and you may struggle to see beyond their spirituality; they may put spirituality before all else, and end up being all about the latest spiritual techniques, or books, or programmes, even at the cost of their friends or family.

Think of someone soulful, however, and it's different.

Soulful people, I tend to find, usually walk with a limp, for a start – because they have been wounded along the way, and have felt pain, but have stopped trying to push it away, and have assimilated it instead into their journey. Some of the most soulful conversations you can have are with people who have suffered tragedy and have not spent the rest of their life trying to run from it but have – in the end – faced into it instead.

My own mind turns to a dear friend, Howard, as a case in point, who is a retired head teacher and who leads retreats with me during springtime (as he's also a botanist). Howard lost his daughter in a car crash when she was little. He was in the car too, and missed her funeral because he was still in a coma, badly injured. In the years that I have known him, Howard has never been afraid to talk about his daughter's death, nor to let us talk about it, even though it clearly brings him pain, and he knows he will never be the same again, having lost her.

He has a gentle sadness that he wears with grace, and which he wouldn't try to hide; yet there is, too, a hopefulness and a joyfulness and a richness to the way he engages with people, which inspires me, and which comes from having faced what he has had to face in life, and in death.

In fact, on a recent retreat we were leading, one participant had recently lost his son to illness. We had been reflecting, as a group, on spring and its themes of new life and hope, and this poor man was finding it to be too much too soon (quite understandably); he had thought the retreat might help, but it was still too raw for him, and tears began to flow.

I had no words of comfort for him – what could I say, without offering platitudes? Yet Howard put an arm around him, and whispered with a gentle authority that while he would never get over losing his child, the pain might ease one day, as it had done for him ... and that he would find hope again within, not despite, his sorrow. This was a moment of extraordinary soulful connection, made possible because Howard allows the seeming opposites of life and death, pain and pleasure, sorrow and joy, to cohere in mysterious unity within him.

This *is* extraordinary wholeness.

There is an earthedness to those who are soulful that makes them approachable and puts them, somehow, within reach. Their journey feels inspiring, their story engaging, and it is usually about struggle more than attainment. And there is a great release for us *all* in that. These are people who contain the mystery; who live within the creative tension. They don't try to push away the darkness, but have stared into it, and have made some peace with it and within it. Through them, we can see the true colours of life, just like the colours of autumn, shining through.

A case study: the fading of the light

And if, as weeks go round, in the dark of the moon
my spirit darkens and goes out, and soft strange
    gloom
pervades my movements and my thoughts and
    words
then I shall know that I am walking still
with God, we are close together now the moon's in
    shadow.

                                D.H. Lawrence, 'Shadows'

We're not all imminently facing death or tragedy (though let's remember how fragile life is, and how many people around us may be facing either of those without our knowing it). Nevertheless, each of us is capable of living in greater wholeness, and more soulfully, day to day. It's not something to be achieved so much as accepted and received. There are many small ways we can embrace wholeness in our daily lives, but here is one example that can lead us more soulfully and colourfully into something we might otherwise prefer to try to keep at bay: the darkness.

Continuing the autumn theme as an example, then, one thing I used to lament when it came to the 'season of mists and mellow fruitfulness' was the fading of the light. I love the long, warm evenings of summer, and all they evoke for me: memories of cricket matches late into the evening, and the lengthening shadows, and the swallows flitting, and the taste of cider, and the smell of cut grass . . . So when autumn arrives, it feels like a very long haul through the months of darkness until we can begin to enjoy that warmth and light of life once more.

It's very easy – because we have done this throughout history – to fear the dark so much that we equate darkness with 'bad' and light with 'good'. We speak of dark days, dark deeds, of our being 'in the dark' . . . and the metaphors have stuck. Our minds love to create those binary opposites to make life easier to judge and to evaluate it, and so we welcome the light, but push away the darkness and label it negatively.

Yet even a quick pause to reflect on this reminds us that we need darkness. Imagine if there were no sunsets, no chance to see the last colours of the afternoon flare and fade, or to feel the first cool breeze of the evening after a hot day, or to see the first star glimmering, or to sink into the luxurious depths of pitch-dark sleep.

At first glance, my own Christian tradition speaks loudly of 'light = good', 'dark = bad'. But it's not as simple as that. In the beginning, we read in Genesis, God said, 'Let there be light!' and there was light, of course, and God 'saw that it was good' – but when he separated the day from the night, he didn't declare that the night was *bad*.

Humanity needed darkness, too, to encounter God. God said to Moses, 'You cannot see my face. For no one may see me and live.' And so when Moses climbed Mount Sinai to meet with God, a dark cloud enveloped the mountain, which, as the episcopal priest and author Barbara Brown Taylor points out, 'reveals the divine presence even while obscuring it'. The Hebrew word for this darkness is *araphel* – which recurs in Psalm 97: 'the Lord reigns, let the Earth rejoice ... Clouds and thick darkness surround him.' The poet Henry Vaughan puts it like this in his intriguing poem 'The Night': 'there is in God ... a deep but dazzling darkness'.

We are conceived in darkness, incubated in darkness, and born from out of the darkness, both literally and spiritually. It is a place of huge promise, then; the promise of new life. A seed, after all, must fall to the ground and die if the life within it is to grow. As the writer and speaker Christine Caine puts it so well, 'Sometimes when you're in a dark place you think you've been buried, but you've actually been planted.'

* * *

During one Advent, I explored this theme of darkness with an online community that included participants from many countries around the world. We asked what it might mean to embrace the natural darkness of encroaching winter, and instead of fearing it learn to welcome and even love it. So we did small exercises such as turning off all our artificial light (through which we seek to keep the dark at bay) for an hour and sitting still, within the natural darkness; we went for walks after dark; and in particular, every night of Advent, we stepped outside to look up at the moon.

It was a moving, unifying and humbling experience, to hear from people all over the world who were stepping out to look up at the same moon, and to think of each other, and to pray within its gentle luminescence.

You don't need to wait for Advent to do this, of course – you could choose one lunar cycle, which is roughly a calendar month, preferably in the autumn or winter, and set aside a short period of time each night to step out into the darkness and locate the moon, and to watch it wax and then wane. Most of us are so disconnected from the rhythms of the moon and stars that we wouldn't know what stage of the lunar cycle we were in, and this is a helpful way to reconnect in some small way to the greater rhythms of which we all form a part.

Let your eyes grow accustomed to the darkness, and you'll find yourself increasingly at home within it. See what you notice without the help of artificial light. You may, perhaps, like to use this as a way of facing into some of the 'darker' times of your life, times when you have experienced pain or loss, and instead of pushing them away, receive them back as part of your own 'hidden wholeness' of which Thomas Merton speaks. Use this time as an outdoor version of the *hygge* exercise I suggested earlier, to help you combine a sense of loving reconnection to the moonlight and natural darkness with an acceptance of a difficult situation. You can use the welcoming prayer to help you with this, too. This needn't be a stark, difficult process though; remember the loveliness of *hygge*: it can be a chance to befriend the darkness. To honour it by not trying to push it away, but to enjoy being out there, looking up at the stars or the moon, when normally you would be inside.

* * *

The aim of the soulful journey is not to be flattened into some kind of spiritual cardboard cut-out with a perma smile and a mindful pose. You are not too good to be true, and you never will be.

You are whole because of your struggle as well as
your success.
I am whole because of the uphill as well as the
down.
We are whole because of the darkness as well as the
light.

I want to learn to walk in the dark as much as the
light ... to be less afraid of that dark and to be more
willing to explore it and to find treasures within it. The
prophet Isaiah wrote of finding 'treasure in the darkness'
and I want, now, to start by believing that this treasure
might indeed be wholeness. And to welcome the peace
that comes through starting from *here*; not in trying to
push away what's difficult, but in travelling into it.

Beauty from ashes

New life, as the writer Barbara Brown Taylor reminds
us, 'starts in the dark. Whether it is a seed in the ground,
a baby in the womb, or Jesus in the tomb, it starts in the
dark.'

My friend Heather is a dear lady with a great love for
the outdoors (she has a gorgeous garden) and a deep
sense of what is soulful. Recently she suffered a debilitating stroke, losing much of the movement on one side
of her body. It dealt her a huge blow (though she never
fails to remind me that there are many other people who
are worse off than her). She's now back to walking a

few paces without a stick, which is encouraging, though she admits to having felt hopeless during some of the bleaker times in her convalescence.

I asked Heather what helped keep her going during her hardest days (and nights), and she replied, unswervingly, that it was one of the Psalms – Psalm 23: 'The Lord is my shepherd, I shall not want ...' There are times in our life when we might feel as if some or even all hope has gone, and during those periods it can be of huge solace to know what touches our soul – whether that's poetry, music, scripture, art – and to hold to those things in faith. Times such as these will often reveal what matters most to our soul, if we are present to them.

But as Heather has begun, slowly, to regain movement, she has also experienced small green shoots of hope for the future. It has taken plenty of time for her even to *begin* to accept what has happened to her. Yet when I asked her whether any sense of goodness has arisen because (and not despite) of her difficult time – 'beauty from ashes' as she then immediately described it, quoting from Isaiah – once again, she did not hesitate.

Her relationship with her two brothers had been helped, she said; they are now much closer, having drifted apart over many years, and are reconciled in a way that would have never happened without the trauma. This was precious to her beyond words.

Second, she said with an inspiring assurance that the fear that had dogged her throughout most of her life has begun to lose its power. She was born in London during an air raid in the Second World War, and her mother was understandably terrified. Heather believes she inherited this fear from her, and admits to having been stalked by fear throughout much of her life. 'But now I have looked death in the eyes, and I know I do not need to fear anything any more,' she told me.

As we chatted, it became clear that she was aware of a growing sense of freedom, since the stroke, that she had not experienced before. She knows she may never regain full movement, and that this would be a terrible loss (there is no hiding from that); yet within all this, she doesn't want to be held back: for even within the physical limitation, she has experienced a different sense of liberation, which hints at a deepening quality of life.

The writer Anne Lamott puts it very touchingly. 'My understanding of incarnation', she writes, 'is that we are not served by getting away from the grubbiness of suffering. Sometimes we feel that we are barely pulling ourselves forwards through a tight tunnel on badly scraped elbows. But we do come out the other side, exhausted and changed.'

16

Finding a soulful rhythm as natural as breathing

We humans are rhythmic creatures; try to listen to an infectiously catchy piece of music, after all, and *not* tap your feet or sway or dance. Rhythm is in our bones and blood. We were born into it; into a natural world of seasons and cycles within which we ourselves experience many seasons and cycles of our own.

It's easy, however, to lose our rhythm in life, and to find ourselves out of sync – painfully so, at times – in a culture in which few of us ever seem willing to pause for long enough to catch our breath before moving on. We try to work as if we're laptop computers that can be switched on first thing in the morning, multi-task like mad until last thing at night, and then set to 'sleep' for a few hours, before doing it all again the next day. Our anxious minds don't want us to stop – there is always more to be done! – so we seldom give ourselves (or each other) permission to be renewed and soulfully restored. We're good at spending energy, but not so good at replenishing it.

The trouble is, we're not computers, or any form of machine for that matter. And the more we try to act like them, the greater our dis-ease will grow. In a culture characterised increasingly by burnout, is it possible for us to rediscover a more soulful rhythm that feels as natural as breathing?

For soulfulness is not about merely finding coping mechanisms with which to survive the week; it's about finding our *groove* – and moving soulfully throughout our days thereafter, as if we were put on Earth for good reason. As the wonderful Maya Angelou once said, 'My mission in life is not merely to survive, but to thrive.'

Rediscovering good sources of energy

What is it like when you feel trapped in a soul*less* rhythm or routine?

Perhaps it feels as if you are merely going through the motions, not truly living; life seems bland or rushed, from your friendships to your mealtimes, and you end up skimming the surface, but no more. Or you may feel as if you're a headless chicken with so many things to do that you can't cope. It's not soulful, for sure. When you want to recharge, you feel almost too tired to face feeding yourself (literally or metaphorically) anything much healthier than junk.

The expert on leadership and energy, Tony Schwartz, believes that the way to find rhythm again is to focus specifically on our personal energy – on the way we spend energy, and the way we renew or recharge our energy. He says that we are oscillatory creatures, whose energy naturally ebbs and flows. We can think about this in terms of how we spend energy positively (which he calls 'performance') or negatively ('survival'). And we can think similarly in terms of how we recharge our energy positively ('renewal') or negatively (when we find ourselves in 'burnout').

One final categorisation: Schwartz argues that we can sub-divide energy into physical energy (the bedrock of all our personal energy, which starts with sleep), mental energy (which helps the focused mind), emotional energy and spiritual energy (the area of values, belief, meaning and purpose; what gets us up in the morning).

The point is that when we find ourselves in the 'performance' zone – spending energy in a positive way, doing perhaps what we feel we've been put on Earth to do – we can only keep going for a certain time before we begin to flag. Our periods of peak energy last for around ninety minutes. And it makes sense! When I'm working I tend, for example, to notice that I'm losing mental energy when I realise I've read the same paragraph five times over without being able to tell you what it said. At this point, we have a choice: stop, to renew our energy positively, or continue to try spending what little energy we have ... but with increasingly negative effect. This is when we move into the 'survival' zone. That's when we might start procrastinating, or taking short-cuts in our work. We tend to make poor decisions in the survival zone, and become tetchy or impatient, and take far longer to complete a simple task (which happens when we stay later and later at work).

After time spent in the survival zone, we simply *have* to try to take energy on board, but we are more likely to try to take on energy in a negative or unhealthy way (and thus we move into the 'burnout' zone). Perhaps we're too tired to cook properly, so we eat junk. We want to numb the pain so we drink a few too many glasses. We surf the social media on our devices while watching late-night TV in a vain attempt to claw back some time for ourselves, and go to bed with unsettled minds and sleep fitfully. And so on. Perhaps you can think of how you personally try to recharge in ways that you know, deep down, are unhealthy or worse.

So we can very easily end up oscillating between survival and burnout, which is a soulless rhythm indeed.

But return in your mind to that point when you were in the performance zone, doing what you do best with energy and focus! You begin to notice you are starting to flag – and *this* is the point at which we can be mindful, awake to the fact that we have a choice. We don't have to keep going endlessly, so that we look busy and assuage our guilt at slacking off. Instead, we have the option of renewing positively, healthily, even just for a short while, in order then to return to the performance zone *renewed*. So how do we find truly restorative ways to recharge our energy, and to develop a rhythm that begins to feel as natural as breathing in and breathing out?

The first thing to say is that it takes courage to stop, especially in a working context, but even, for example, if you are a home-maker who feels guilty about taking a break from the chores. Our egos do push us ever onwards, and to flourish soulfully we need to break that cycle. It may seem courageous to keep going no matter what, but the bravest decision is to look after yourself, and to renew physically, mentally, emotionally and spiritually.

It helps to develop small habits that enable you to oscillate between spending and renewing your energy positively, so that in the end you don't have to think too hard about them. If you work for long periods at a desk, this might involve focusing hard for forty-five minutes (and if possible turning off e-mail or Internet during this time, thus preserving mental energy, which is depleted with every interruption) and performing what Schwartz calls a 'sprint'. You could even set an alarm and stick to this time limit, to help you to form the habit, and to develop a rhythm of working with true focus. It does not hurt to stop, even if you are 'on a roll'.

Give yourself a complete change of scene, even if for a few short minutes. Get up, move around physically, get outside if you possibly can, talk to another human being (instead of texting or e-mailing), read a newspaper instead of reading a website, and so on. At lunchtime, you might start by actually taking a lunch break, eating healthy food away from your desk, going for a longer walk or a run, getting to a gallery or doing something that lifts you emotionally and spiritually, and in the evening, you might try going home on time, and eating well, seeing people, and getting a proper night's sleep. For instance.

If you are able to form a habit over a season such as Lent, during which so many of us grant ourselves permission to give certain bad habits up and to develop new and positive ones, then so much the better, because a run of twenty-one days or more is enough to retrain yourself effectively.

When I've explored this with others in workshops, I've found that most people are easily able to describe what they are doing, and how they are feeling, when they are in survival or burnout. It's a place we all recognise. But we tend to find it harder to come up with positive ways to renew, because that's the area we neglect the most. Life throws so many seemingly *urgent* things at us that we do not allow ourselves time for what is *important* to us. So, increasingly, we lose touch with what truly energises us.

There is no need to despair, however: new, healthier and sustainable rhythms are within reach, and I'd like now to consider how we might recharge and renew in ways that can, overall, help us to develop a more soulful rhythm to life.

* * *

Before you read on, then, perhaps you would return your attention to your breathing, that most fundamental of rhythms. Become aware of it once more. Relax, follow your in-breath all the way to its end, then follow the out-breath, and do this a few times, to remind yourself of how powerful this can be. Notice again whether you have any tension in your body, and as you relax into a deeper peace, settle back into your soul.

* * *

I'd like, then, to ask how we might find soulful renewal within each of the four categories of energy in turn: physical, mental, emotional and spiritual. We'll start with the bedrock of all our energy, the physical.

How do you renew physically, in a positive way?

As Tony Schwartz argues, sleep is the most fundamental way to restore ourselves physically, and most of us don't get enough of it. Yet this is something that is completely within reach (unless you suffer from insomnia, of course, or have babies or young children).

To enjoy a soulfully satisfying night's sleep, it's worth not just getting to bed earlier, but to have a pause from TV before you go to sleep. You might try the Examen exercise we mentioned earlier, and review your day with gratitude. Or simply spend a short time in stillness.

Consider, too, the physical 'space' you sleep in. How restful is it? How many electrical devices do you keep in the room (do you charge your phone there?), and which ones are still receiving incoming mail or providing social media alerts that will beep and buzz? Even the smallest light, such as a computer 'sleep mode' light, is likely to affect the quality of your sleep. Remember Barbara Brown Taylor's invitation to embrace the natural darkness: how dark is your room, and how can you give yourself the best chance to restore your energy most deeply and profoundly?

So many of us put sleep at the bottom of the list – often, again, out of bravado. We like to think we'll get extra points for sending e-mails to colleagues in the early hours. But this is a culture we would do well to break, and to give each other permission to break, in order to honour true rest.

Eating and drinking provides us with physical energy, of course, and so you might consider healthier ways to eat and drink throughout the day. How much water are you taking on, for instance, and when? Can you become more intentional about the times you have a pit stop to refuel? Remembering how mindlessly we can 'use' tea and coffee to stimulate us (in survival mode!), be mindful of the way you are drinking, and develop healthy pauses, proper breaks, in which to savour the drink instead of throwing it down your throat while on the go.

We also touched upon eating mindfully, in Part 1, becoming more present to our food – pausing to breathe before we eat, and to be thankful, and to taste each mouthful slowly: this all helps us to appreciate the goodness set before us. And this takes us further into soulful territory. For food and drink certainly bring people together powerfully, and that's why a small group of us always gather around my kitchen table for a monthly soulful gathering. There is something in the act of eating and drinking that creates a nourishing context in which to be fed in all sorts of other ways, too.

If we combine the mindfulness of the pause with the soulfulness of the loving reconnection – with the food itself, with the people, with the place – then a certain soul space can open within our schedule, too: a chance to breathe in before proceeding onwards with soul and grace as we continue with the day.

As a matter of personal indulgence, there is rarely anything more soulful for me than to eat a crumble made from the apples that have been picked from the tree in our garden. They've been a year in the making, after all. I pruned the tree in winter. I watched the smallest leaves arrive in specks of fresh green in early spring. I saw blossom bud and then burst into clouds of pink and white. Small apples began to swell through the summer, ripening in the sunshine into their final display of ruddy-cheeked autumnal fulsomeness.

And then, as a family, we picked them – me wobbling in the upper branches and the kids below, catching the fruit in a laundry basket as I lobbed it down. That very act in itself fed us soulfully as a group.

But then the crumble itself! There is *surely* nothing quite like cooking or tasting what you have grown, picked or foraged (I confess, my wife is the cook), nor giving some away to bless others (when did you last receive a home-cooked meal from a friend, and how did that make you feel?), or inviting friends or neighbours to sit with you and share in the eating.

What might it look like for you, to take on physical energy in a mindful and soulful way that not only gives you fuel for the journey, but releases you into more deeply satisfying rhythms of life?

* * *

When it comes to *mental* energy, there is great potential for finding more of a soulful rhythm if you maintain a little discipline. This can involve simplifying your physical environment (tidying, decluttering, to create a cleaner and more inspiring space in which to work, for example) as well as stripping out any potential interference when you are focusing mentally on one task. Short interruptions, such as a text or an incoming e-mail, can cost a disproportionate amount of time if our concentration is broken; never mind our habit of surfing the Internet when we start to get bored or distracted. Stepping outside for some fresh air, or walking across to speak to a colleague instead of 'messaging' them, can restore mental energy, and reconnect us soulfully.

As I said above, setting time limits can help you to establish a rhythm and a flow to the day. Work in shorter bursts while keeping e-mail and phones off, so that you can focus all your mental energy for a limited time on one task only, before stopping to catch your breath. By factoring in regular pauses and breaks, we can use these to stay present to what we are doing; for me, writing in shorter bursts provides an opportunity, each time I stop, to remember to savour the process (one thing at a time, lovingly, remember!), instead of wishing I was finished already. Especially if I combine that pause with a few moments outside, to breathe the air, and listen to the birds, and to remember that the whole of life is sacred, including the 'work'.

*　　*　　*

At the *emotional* level, one simple soulful way to renew is with times of appreciation or thankfulness. If we learn to factor this into the rhythm of our day – pausing to count our blessings, stopping to appreciate the smallest gifts, or even just remembering to thank people for what they do – then not only does gratitude rise in our hearts, but it soon overflows to those around us, too.

A simple way to do this more intentionally is to keep a gratitude diary, in which you record bullet points (three per day is helpful) that allow you to go back in search of 'what went well' instead of 'what went wrong'. By doing this, you can train your brain to look for goodness wherever you find yourself, even within the most difficult situations. You might like to do this in the pause before you go to bed.

Perhaps you are not very good at receiving – whether that's receiving help, or compliments, or feedback ... But other people will energise you, if you let them. So, accepting the advice of a friend, or acknowledging that you cannot do something on your own, is a powerful step in nurturing collaboration with others, which is hugely beneficial, emotionally, to both parties. I am still working on this; but recently when I dared to ask a friend for help in pulling down a section of ceiling that needed replastering, not only did he express delight that I had asked him, but as we engaged in the physical labour of it all, we were both renewed emotionally. We loved working together. The camaraderie brought us closer, and I felt blessed to receive the kind of help that more than lightened the load.

The psychologist and happiness expert Shawn Achor advocates performing random acts of kindness as a way of yielding a palpable sense of emotional well-being – not just for the recipient, but for the one being kind. Whether that's offering a lift, cooking a meal for someone, helping a stranger or paying for the person behind you in the queue when you're at the coffee shop, for instance, it all helps to restore your own emotional energy.

In fact, it's one of five things, according to Achor, which – if you implement them consistently for twenty-one days – will bring a more powerful sense of positivity into the present. The other four involve keeping a gratitude diary, meditating, journalling a positive experience, and exercise.

Exercise certainly yields great emotional energy for me (even though I am spending physical energy in the process!). When I go for a run, it resets me; I always return feeling happier and healthier, and having restored something of my connection with God as well as nature in the process.

I love the fact that the Japanese consider walking in the woods to be a preventative form of medicine. It's known as *shinrin-yoku*, or 'forest bathing' – what a beautiful phrase – which the author Robert Penn says is not only emotionally but physically good for you, because it reduces heart rate and blood pressure, decreases sympathetic nerve activity and lowers levels of the stress hormone cortisol. It is all interlinked.

* * *

When it comes to *spiritual* energy, I mean drawing from anything that brings meaning and purpose, and helps us to see the bigger picture (along with our own place within it) more clearly, so that we know why we're doing what we're doing. You can draw great spiritual energy from having a strong sense of vocation, for instance. You may not get paid for the voluntary work that you do in the community, but you know why you're doing it, and it energises you in a deep and fulfilling way.

Faith, and everything that comes with it – belief, prayer, worship and so forth – is, of course, a great source of spiritual energy. Try reading Psalm 23, for example, like Heather – slowly and carefully, and let it speak to you and restore you. You could take yourself off on a retreat, whether that's to an organised one you've seen online, or to a monastery on your own for a day, or simply an afternoon with your journal and a good long walk. You could fast for a day, which is a powerful complement to the soulful act of feasting. Fasting reminds us that we do not 'live on bread alone', as Jesus once said. It helps me, I find, to become more keenly aware of that sense of soul friendship between my true self and God, deep within. You might observe 'seasons' such as Lent or Advent, and throw yourself into them creatively. My friend Paula creates amazing journals during both of those seasons, with photos, cuttings, sketches, mind-maps and the like. Her creativity reminds and inspires me to be dynamically creative in my response to life and faith!

But spiritual energy doesn't have to flow exclusively from the classically spiritual sources; for me personally, it arrives just as powerfully, if not more sometimes, through poetry, music and art. So beware of thinking of the arts as an indulgence, or *merely* as a hobby.

I've worked with people who acknowledge that poetry feeds them most deeply; yet they have struggled, nevertheless, to set aside regular time to read even just one poem during the course of their day, because they are busy, or because it can feel like an indulgence when there are so many other seemingly more 'urgent' tasks to complete; but if it feeds your soul, if it fills you with passion, if it fires your creativity or connects you to a bigger picture, if it gets you thinking in a different way or helps you to relax, if it inspires new ideas ... then what *on earth* is indulgent about it? You wouldn't berate yourself for eating healthily, for feeding yourself an apple instead of a packet of sweets. So when it comes to soul food, why shouldn't a poem a day – if it feeds you – become a staple part of your diet?

This does, of course, mean that we may have to stop doing something else in order to free up the time – which is a disciplined way to open up a soulful space. If we stop wasting time and energy mindlessly surfing the Internet, for example, we will almost undoubtedly find space to spend with our anthology.

This is where mental energy also feeds into the spiritual: it's helpful to read a poem (since we're talking about poetry) in an environment that's conducive to soaking it in. Even if it's just for five minutes, we can switch off the phone, close the door, make ourselves comfortable, and honour the process, as if it were a sacred act. For it *is* a sacred act.

Give yourself to the poem, instead of expecting the poem to give something to you. Be present to each word, each line, and make a little space either side of reading it – even if it's just thirty seconds of intentional pause

– to ensure this is not done 'on the run'. Your soul will draw deep, the poetry will enter your bloodstream, and the chances are, the way you think, and speak, and act, will become an extension of that poetry, and your day will be blessed with a poetic quality all of its own.

Sweet soul music

There's surely a reason why the best kind of music tends to be called soul music, isn't there?

The singer Bono refers, in an inspiring introduction he once wrote to *The Book of Psalms*, to the way music has a power all of its own. And he's not talking, in particular, about church music, but 'the honesty of John Lennon, the baroque language of Bob Dylan and Leonard Cohen, the open throat of Al Green and Stevie Wonder'.

'When I hear these singers,' he says, 'I am reconnected to a part of me I have no explanation for – my "soul" I guess.'

Perhaps this is true for you, too. I wonder when you last listened to a piece of music, not to fill the background void, but for the sake of it, as a work of art that touches you and blesses you and stretches and inspires you in equal measure. Again, the context can matter: if we switch out the lights, or sit in a favourite chair, or even take our music outside with headphones into one of Oliver Buerkeman's so-called 'thin places' . . . then we are sometimes better placed to receive. And just as we can listen with soul to people, so too, surely, for music and the arts in general: tuning in to each note, feeling the rhythm, being lifted on the melodies, and inspired by the poetry of lyrics or libretto. Reconnected to that part of us that we have 'no explanation for'.

*   *   *

The renewal zone is where we draw deep, therefore. It reminds me of the words from Psalm 42, which says, 'As the deer pants for streams of water, so my soul pants for you.' The psalmist was writing about his deep thirst for God, but we surely all have a deep and soulful longing for 'more'. I like to think of this zone, where we can find restoration, as the source of our renewal . . . It's where we can return to, to draw deep.

But as we reflect, for ourselves, on what constitutes the source, let's remember that it takes courage to get back there. Even though the burnout zone is unpleasant, we take comfort from staying there. We get used to soul-less rhythms, even though our soul keeps calling to us to remind us that there are better rhythms to find. So it takes courage to leave that zone and to step into a different kind of rhythm. And it takes time and space to discover the source of soulful renewal.

One exercise I have done for myself is to trace a river to its source, and to use this opportunity to reflect upon where I draw strength and energy from in my own life. It felt like a very special time when I headed out to follow the stream 'upwards'. Ever narrowing, it reversed up a little waterfall and into stillness: and there was a wide-ish pool, where freshly surfaced waters seemed to be gathering for their journey; the aquamarine glassiness hinting of the chalk aquifers deep below, through which they had filtered so steadily for years, and from which they had so recently been released. Immediately behind the pool, the merest trace of a channel, retreating further up the hillside and into the mulch of undergrowth, before disappearing almost entirely from view, harder and harder to discern now, save for the fountain – there! – springing like a miracle, clean from the ground: the source.

Why not trace the source of a river or stream for yourself? When you find it, spend a little time there counting your breath, being present to the scene itself, and allowing it to speak to you at a soulful level. Imagine a source beginning to flow within you. If you don't have time to trace a source, you could at least get to a river and walk a short stretch of it upstream. Use this as a walking meditation (relaxing, paying attention to your breathing and your steps as you go) to embody your intention to return to the source of love and life; to the source of your own soulful energy.

The 'source' helps to symbolise, for me, everything about the process of renewal and restoration. I know that I need to return to it regularly, to breathe in – literally and figuratively – to be 'inspired'. To draw deep, to find space, to reconnect, so that I am able to give flesh-and-blood expression to this inner aliveness I call soul, and to reach out to the world around me in love.

Start by breathing in, from a place of contentment

A final word on rhythm. I believe there's a direct relationship between drawing deeply from what's soulfully restorative and *acting* within the world in a soulful way ourselves. We breathe in to breathe out.

But there's something about the position we start from that is worth remembering. Shawn Achor argues powerfully that in Western culture, we believe that happiness and contentment only ever follows 'success' – and so we keep working harder in order to try to be successful, in order to be happy. The trouble is, whenever we *are* 'successful' (however you might define success, which is open to debate), we tend to move the goalposts: so if you hit your sales target, the company doesn't throw a party, it increases your sales target for next month! In this way, happiness and contentment remain forever out of reach. This helps us to explain why we never really pause for breath.

Yet Achor's research shows that we work most creatively and productively – and I would suggest soulfully – when we *begin* from a place of contentment, not striving. In fact, the brain is up to 31 per cent more creative and productive when it's starting not from a place of what Achor calls 'neutral, negative or stressed', but from 'positive'.

This resonates for me so powerfully with what Jesus said when he spoke these words to his followers: 'Do not worry about your life, what you will eat or drink; or about your body, what you will wear. Is not life more than food, and the body more than clothes? ... Do not worry about tomorrow.'

I love the way Eugene Peterson translates this in his paraphrase of the Bible, *The Message*: 'What I'm trying to do here is to get you to relax, to not be so preoccupied with getting, so you can respond to God's giving.'

We can return to our most simple mindful practice to remind us of this, time and again: whenever we begin a project or piece of work, or start a task or 'chore'; whenever we sit down to listen deeply to someone, or go on a journey; whenever we contemplate our future, we can start by taking a deep breath. It's called *inspiration*.

17

Soulful expression through our life's work

How do you express yourself soulfully?

When I asked this question on social media, one lady immediately replied, 'By pouring out my heart through poetry.' I love that answer.

It might indeed, for you, be through writing, or perhaps painting, or cooking; soulful expression is likely to be creative. You might express yourself through design, architecture, technology or singing. One person told me that if they haven't been able to sing carols in the run-up to Christmas, the season does not feel the same; they cannot connect with it in the same way. At home, I know when my wife is feeling joyful because she starts to sing around the house. Singing connects her to life, and without doubt is an overflow of her soul.

We have to make space for the soul to express itself, however. If we are too worried about what others will think of us, and we're more concerned about pleasing or impressing others than finding a true, authentic expression of our own, then we will stifle its flow. We won't be as imaginative, for fear of being shot down. We may not take the creative risk we need to, or try something new. This is a great danger for most of us individually – and the danger collectively is that we flatten each other out into pale versions of who we really could be. In the end, culture suffers. The world suffers! It's therefore crucial to open up space between us for the soul to find its voice, and to give permission, both to ourselves and to others, to let the soul sing.

Let your soul sing

In this regard, I take great inspiration from the skylark, the herald of spring. For the skylark sings with a freedom that might encourage us.

In fact, it sings up to an astonishing 200 separate notes or consonants *per second*, according to David Hindley, who used to be head of music at Homerton College, Cambridge, and who recorded and slowed down the bird's song to study it. He discovered that fifty seconds' worth of skylark can be transposed into thirteen minutes of sheet-music; and that, remarkably, the structures of its music closely resemble those of Beethoven's Fifth Symphony.

All the while, the skylark never sings the same thing twice. It is forever composing unique variations – new every morning! – which are, says Mr Hindley, 'on equal terms with anything man has ever written'. 'Profuse strains', as the poet Shelley puts it in his ode 'To a Skylark', 'of unpremeditated art'.

And Shelley's choice of the word 'unpremeditated' is significant, I believe. We're not all great composers, nor skylarks, but nevertheless a soulful creativity *can* flow uniquely through us, too, like the lark-song, if we manage not to worry so much about what others think of our efforts, or whether we're good enough. We have a unique voice, a melody, creativity, but to hear it, we must first grant permission for the soul to sing.

I wonder what is stopping you from expressing yourself creatively. Perhaps you even catch yourself saying, 'I'm not a creative person.' It might have been something that your parents or a teacher told you long ago, which meant you lost all confidence. It might have been living in the shadow of a seemingly more talented friend or sibling. It might be that, once, you showed a friend a poem, or sang a song in public, and you were laughed at, or didn't get the reception you were hoping for.

It's easy to laugh at the self-deluded and seemingly talentless participants on TV talent shows, and of course there's a time and a place for recognising that, yes, I am tone deaf (if indeed you are). That shouldn't stop us singing from our soul, however, or finding other ways to craft a really soulful expression – ways that are more suited to our gifts, and that will provide a channel for our own unique creative expression.

We are not all destined for fame, of course, and it doesn't do us much good to seek it for the sake of it. I used to play in bands when I was younger, and we were pretty good, attracting some attention from record companies. While we were focused on getting a record deal, however, it could feel stressful and inhibiting. When we faced up to the fact, in the end, that we were not quite going to get that deal – but decided to continue anyway, simply for the love of playing music together – we discovered a sense of joy that had often been missing from our rehearsals. Some of the happiest and most soulful times flowed once we were making music for the sheer joy of making music together.

*   *   *

The author Robert Bresson writes, 'Make visible what, without you, might never have been seen.' Our calling is not to make visible what we think will wow our peers, or what we believe other people expect of us. Instead, it's to bring into expression the very uniqueness with which we ourselves have been blessed; to offer something of the eternal nature of our soul, creatively, practically, with vulnerability and in love.

So we have a responsibility to bring to bear what's within us – to give expression to our unique, inner aliveness. Yet this is not meant to be burdensome. A friend of mine once told me that there's nothing she has done in her life that could not have been accomplished by someone else. And in a sense I'm sure she's right, just as there's nothing I've done that someone else couldn't have done, too.

Yet my friend has a *way* of doing what she does that perhaps she does not recognise for herself, but that I, and surely many others, do – so that while any number of people could take over her job and continue the role seamlessly, nevertheless, there is no one who could do her job in quite the way she does it. We all make visible something of our own unique soul in the process of connecting lovingly with our work and the people we serve.

She is also a poet, and her poetry has touched me and I'm sure plenty of others. Of course, I could read any number of poets, and each would offer 'poetry' of one kind or another; but my friend is able to express the way she sees the world uniquely and movingly through her own way of writing, and in that sense, she is wrong: *no one* else could have accomplished what she has done.

*   *   *

To help release more of your own creativity, you could start small, by reconnecting with a creative project that you have been putting off (perhaps you have been too busy, or it has felt too indulgent, or you have been afraid to express yourself). While it may not be 'urgent', try to see it as *significant*, nevertheless, because your creative flow is important. It will give you opportunity to connect, to express, to create, to participate in life soulfully, and to breathe something into life that may otherwise not have been witnessed.

What is that you would like to do?
What's stopping you from starting?

Here is another suggestion I have found helpful. Write a poem, lovingly and carefully, but once you have completed it, destroy it. In this way, you are not writing for the sake of receiving praise, nor are you seeking validation for your creativity from anyone else. The poem may be good, or it may be poor, but that's not the point in this instance; instead, savour the process of creation alone. Pour yourself into it, and allow your soul to express something more of itself through the words you choose, but do not let the prospect of sharing your poem inhibit you. As you read it through and then finally tear it up (or even burn it!), enjoy the freedom that comes with opening up this creative channel, and use this exercise as a way of loosening your grip on your need for validation.

Let go, to let come

Sometimes, we need to let go of something – or even have it removed from us – in order to stop perpetuating a soulless cycle, and to release a more soulful expression of who we are in the world.

My friend Linda is a case in point. For several years, she worked hard for a large NGO that was helping the poor, the marginalised and the dispossessed around the world. It's what Linda believed in, and it seemed very much like the 'right' thing to do. The only problem was, she didn't always feel as if she was fully flourishing within that environment – which is hard to admit when your work is compassionate, and is making a difference.

Linda had always loved baking. In her spare time, she began to run a very small part-time baking enterprise from her house, making cupcakes, which she called 'Filled With Love'. One day, quite unexpectedly (and causing much shock), she was made redundant from the charity; but after recovering from her initial disorientation, Linda held her nerve: for she had sensed something stirring in her soul for some time, which the redundancy seemed to confirm. She felt that *this* was the time and the opportunity for her love of baking to find true expression in her life.

So instead of looking by default for the security of a like-for-like job, she took a risk on soul, and poured her energies – and her love, crucially! – into cupcakes. Within a year or so, she had moved into premises, creating a café space she called 'The Kitchen', which has now become a community hub. This is what she wrote to me about it:

I have seen what this place – The Kitchen – is doing for the community and the people who live here. Young mums meet together and receive wisdom from those who went through it all many years ago. People on their own, or elderly couples looking for somewhere to go and 'get out for an hour' bring a book and sit by the window watching the world go by.

Yes – I used to think that working to alleviate poverty was the highest calling. And of course there are times when I look at the indulgences offered in a cake shop and think of the cocoa farmers who grow our chocolate, or the vanilla growers who work so hard in such difficult circumstances, but for whom Fairtrade is offering hope.

Every day we have conversations with people in The Kitchen, ranging from sleepless babies to school places to how to transform our community and nation. We believe we are building community here and our hope is that everyone who visits us will leave happier and more able to face whatever life throws at them.

I've come to see that there are different ways of changing the world. Instead of doing what I felt I ought to do I have followed my gut, my passion – my soul, I guess. It's not always been easy, of course; but I feel a sense of everything I have done in my life so far leading me to this point, and of being where I was meant to be.

Linda's story very powerfully helps to encapsulate what 'soulful expression' can look like. We see that it's not easy. The pull towards what we feel we 'ought' to do is strong. There is risk in following the path of soul. But if you stop to notice, you will sense its leading. She described it as following her gut, her passion, 'my soul, I guess'. And I would say she displayed great courage by responding to that leading. The upshot is a sense that this is where she was meant to be.

And she has created the kind of soul space around her, physically in the form of the café, which invites others to step into her space and to flourish. She's a wonderful example, then, of making soul space, quite literally.

From my personal experience, it was when my own plans fell through that I seemed better able to sense the soul's leading, because I became more open to what *could* happen next instead of what *should*. I'd had to loosen my grip on what I thought the future ought to hold, and once I did, I experienced a sense of creative flow that touched many areas of my life. When the ego doesn't have a clue what to do next, the soul has a fighting chance of taking the lead, if we yield. That's when it's well worth tuning right in and paying heed to the nudge.

Work is love made visible

The fact that Linda called her enterprise 'Filled With Love' is significant. Kahlil Gibran writes that 'Work is love made visible', which is an inspiring statement for any of us who are keen to explore what soulful expression might look like through the 'work' of our life. Our life's work, whether we are paid to do it or not.

Love is the benchmark for soul work, in fact, because love, ultimately, as we have considered, is the benchmark for soul.

Similarly, the poet Rumi writes: 'Let the beauty of what you love, be what you do.'

It's hard to love the daily grind (though we can positively make our peace with whatever we're involved with, of course) – but to see our work as 'love made visible' releases us, perhaps, from becoming defined solely by our roles in life, and it means we can always give expression to what we might call our soul work, whether or not it is what we are paid to do, or whether it is acknowledged as an official role or title. You may not have had a job for some time, and that can feel disempowering – but again, you need not be defined in terms of what you do not have.

Through soulful expression, we can each become fulltime co-workers for the greater cause of Love. While the rhythm of ego is, perhaps, to take for ourselves, and to consume, and to dispose of, and to come back for more, the rhythm of soul provides a mutually beneficial exchange.

*   *   *

I love the way the cultural anthropologist Angeles Arrien helps to keep our feet on the ground when it comes to the relationship between soulful ideals and their flesh-and-blood manifestation. (For it's easy to get carried away with lofty ideals, and disappear into the realm of nice ideas, especially when it comes to discussing something as hard to define as soul.) In considering the dynamic relationship between our inner and outer life, between essence and form, she sums it up rather beautifully: 'We walk the mystical path with practical feet.'

This captures the idea of soulfulness so succinctly. It is, indeed, a mystical path, from the moment we pause to let our chattering minds quieten and awaken to the presence we call soul, deeper within; through that inner journey, we press in to discover more and become more of who we truly are, our soulful self, which links us to the infinite and forever brings an eternal dimension to bear on the way we see the present here and now ...

And yet, we must then reach out, in loving connection, and give outward expression to this inward journey: we must *always* walk this path with practical feet!

Remember, we are not aiming to become holier than thou and a little too good to be true. Neither are we seeking escape to Nirvana, while the world goes to hell. It's the soil in our nails, and sometimes, even, the blisters on our feet, that helps us to cultivate the work of soul.

A few exemplars spring to mind immediately of those who walked that mystical path with practical feet. Gandhi was compelled to bring political and social transformation non-violently (often through the literal act of walking, of course). Mother Teresa's spiritual wisdom gained its extraordinary power from the overflow of her practical actions, and vice versa.

And then there's Jesus, of course, whose feet took him into the desert for forty days (which we remember during Lent), before his public work commenced; feet that would have been scorched and callused. Feet that would take him, after those dusty days, back into so many different lives and contexts. He showed, by walking it himself, that the path is both inward *and* outward; and he walked it with such courage and compassion that his feet would bear the scars of crucifixion, in the end, to prove it.

'The way to your heart begins with your feet on the ground,' writes the inspirational priest and author Cynthia Bourgeault: 'Quietly but intensely present.' Perhaps you'd consider your own feet for a few moments, and ask where they could carry you today, and to whom. Especially if you, like me, tend to get excited about ideas but don't always turn them into action.

To embed this idea, try to walk more slowly and mindfully towards the next situation you face. Wherever you are going, be mindful of the way your feet touch the ground, try to move with a little more poise and balance, and as they carry you, consider the impact that your presence can have on the people and the place you are going to.

What can you do, practically, to bless those you are going to see next? Consider one way that you can make a helpful difference, and do it. It might only be making someone a cup of tea to cheer them up. It could be bringing a gift. It could be that you will listen with full and deep attention. But this fourth part of the book is all about embodying soul, expressing your unique inner aliveness through loving connection to the world: so remember that soulfulness is utterly grounded, both in the here and now, and in the realm of practical action.

Trust yourself – others do

One crucial aspect of working, and walking, with soul is to learn to trust our self more fully as we go. But that's never easy.

Your ego doesn't want to trust you. It's worried that you'll mess up, so it wants to grab the controls of your life with a vice-like grip and not let go. (And you're not alone in this, by the way – 'being found out', for instance, is identified as a top-ten fear among CEOs.) The voice that pipes up when we're about to do something – which perhaps says, 'Don't mess this up!' or 'You were never any good at this!' or 'What are you playing at?' – causes us to tense up physically and not act naturally; it's like an anxious companion who is constantly worried that we are going to fail, so keeps trying to take over and tell us what to do while we're trying to do it. It fills the space that our soul needs to breathe and to express itself.

But think for a moment of someone you trust to do a really good job. (You may secretly feel envious of them, but that's another story!) It might be a work colleague or a friend; whoever it is, just think of the trust you would place in them to walk into an appropriate situation and do themselves proud.

Now, it's very likely there are people who feel the same about you, who trust you to do a beautiful job and are confident that you will.

So choose a time when you need to do something you feel nervous about, or are worried about doing wrong, and tell yourself, this time, it's *OK*: if others trust me in this situation, I will trust my soulful self to do what it does best.

I have done this when I am anxious about a situation I'm facing. It might be that I'm going into an organisation to run a workshop, for instance, and I'm worried about what people will think of me, how I will come across, the usual kind of concerns. Of course, just being mindful of that anxious chatter itself is half the battle, and to breathe and relax and enter the situation with open-hearted presence is a great thing.

It still takes some doing, however, to trust yourself within the moment to act well and to respond appropriately. The likelihood is that you *are* fully equipped to do what you do best, otherwise you wouldn't have been invited to do it in the first place. So this is an opportunity for you to trust your deeper instincts, your whole self, and to bless the people you are working for through seeking to serve them in the way only you can, instead of simply trying to impress them.

What happens when you trust yourself? You relax, and give your soul the space and freedom it needs to find expression.

You do not have to sell your soul to join an organisation

Honestly. Please hear me out. Because usually, and depressingly, it's within organisations that we can end up feeling most disempowered, fenced in by other people's rules and goals, and ground down by a pain-fully soul*less* corporate routine. Machine-like and toxic, organisations can fast become 'ego-systems' and little more, as leadership expert Otto Scharmer likes to put it.

In fact, in the ways we've conducted business and organised the world, it sometimes feels as if we believe we've made a pact with the devil: if you want to have a 'successful' life in work and business, there *has* to be a pay-off. It's a zero-sum game. You have to sell your soul to get where you really want to be.

But do you? In the Bible, while the human story starts in a garden, it ends in a city. Can't the way we organise ourselves – and conduct our business – become a soulful expression of human collaboration, too? Can't our organisations become very much a part of the solution instead of the problem?

Frederic Laloux believes so. He's a former strategy consultant with McKinsey & Company, and demonstrates, through the meticulous research of fifteen pioneering organisations (including a school, a healthcare provider and an auto-parts manufacturer), that they can indeed become a soulful expression of their community. He has identified three defining characteristics in particular of these new 'soulful' organisations, as he describes them: self-management (instead of a top-down authority and hierarchy), a sense of evolutionary (not fixed) purpose (which grows organically, as the organisation tunes in, soulfully, to its purpose!), and wholeness.

Wholeness, in an organisational setting, involves finding a new collective rhythm to working, including gathered times of storytelling (a chance to share good news from within the organisation, which normally gets neglected or ignored), collective periods of silence, deeper listening, times of group meditation, appreciative enquiry (looking together for the best of what is, and seeking to build upon strengths and gifts), peer coaching (drawing the best out of each other day by day, instead of waiting for an annual appraisal and the obligatory training course), and environmental integrity.

It's very exciting: imagine collaborating within a soulful environment in which you derive a sense of meaning and purpose from your work, and understand how what you do fits in with the wider whole, and how your organisation is making a difference in the world for good. One radical idea that Laloux highlights is the way some of the organisations he has studied refuse to see themselves as having 'competitors'; after all, if the idea is to achieve the purpose of the organisation, and if others share that purpose, then why not collaborate with other people and organisations, even with the so-called competition?

An organisation I have been working with (which is involved in manufacturing) has been trying hard to model 'wholeness', inspired by the work of Laloux and by some elements of both mindfulness and contemplative spirituality. On the team-building days that I have facilitated over the last three years, we have grown used to practising extended periods of silence, sharing good news stories, and even walking an outdoor labyrinth regularly. (A labyrinth is an ancient form of walking meditation using a path that looks a little like a maze, along which you cannot get lost. You walk in silence, towards the centre, and then out again, an outward expression of the inner soulful journey.)

It took a few sessions for the leadership team – comprising a typical mix of people and backgrounds – to grow accustomed to this way of working together, and our first few sessions were not without their awkward moments and sceptical frowns ... yet in time, the team found itself better able to settle into this deeper way of working together, and of tuning in to each other and to the evolving, emerging purpose of the organisation.

We experienced remarkable synchronicity one afternoon, for instance, when we were exploring the organisation's values again from scratch. The team took an hour or so to walk a labyrinth in silence before regrouping, each of us tasked with selecting five values from a much wider 'menu' we had originally developed. As we wrote down our five choices in advance of a discussion, and revealed them in turn, we discovered there was near unanimous agreement on the final set; the act of walking silently together helped the team to find collective agreement without even needing to speak!

It takes great leadership and courage for (in this instance) the chair to take his team on such a journey as this; but it also takes great courage for the team itself to engage in this kind of practice, and requires an openness to try new things, and a willingness to step together into the unknown, in order to become something greater than the sum of the parts. In order, I believe, to find its collective soul.

As one of Laloux's interviewees has put it: 'Business can produce food, cure disease, control population, employ people, and generally enrich our lives. And it can do these good things and make a profit *without losing its soul*.' We do not necessarily have to lose or sell our soul to make a difference within an organisation; in fact, in the right setting, we can *find* and express our soul through our life's work instead.

If ever we needed soulful organisations, it is now. This does of course require soulful leaders to awaken, to show the way. And as we near the end of this particular beginning, this book, I would like to plant the seed that each one of us can lead with soul, wherever we find ourselves, at such a uniquely challenging and yet opportune time . . .

18

Let the soul take the lead

'A great deal depends, perhaps our humanity
depends, on our sensing and acknowledging that
quality in our kind we call the soul.' Marilynne
Robinson, *The Givenness of Things*

In his recent powerful book *Want More*, the photogra-
pher Alex Schneideman presented a series of photographs of jaded shoppers in seemingly soulless
consumer settings – on crowded streets, jostling in
malls, queuing in stores. Commenting on the pictures
in an accompanying essay, the environmental journalist and poet Harry Eyres wrote about what he saw
inscribed on the faces of those shoppers: 'sullen resig-
nation ... sour dissatisfaction; sadness; boredom;
preoccupation; distraction; sheer misery; panic; grim

determination; utter exhaustion; passivity; dreamy escapism; regression'.

Running throughout Schneideman's photographs is an overwhelming sense of strain, Eyres states. You might identify with that. Yet despite this, he also notices hints of 'the unused powers of humanity' (what an excellent phrase), including the potential for joy, love, care, creativity, and altruism, all of which feel strangely present, he notes, despite the bleakness.

'If people had no souls,' concludes Harry Eyres, 'their faces would not show such resistance; they would simply go with the inhuman flow.'

If people had no souls ... It's a scary thing to imagine, when you stop to think of it, isn't it? Imagine a completely soulless world. Spend a few moments now, if you would, contemplating the prospect.

What would you be missing, if you lived entirely without soul?

*   *   *

But we are not soulless, and when the soul calls to us, whether it's in those fleeting moments of awakening (the 'hints of congruence', which Eugene Peterson speaks of), or whether it's as we step more intentionally into the rhythm of soul that was ours to discover all along, we remember that there *is* more to life than mere consuming and taking, and that the soul will never let us forget it, and it will push up like a flower through the cracks in the concrete paving of our life, and it is still there, etched on the faces of those who find themselves within even the most seemingly soulless of situations. The soul calls, if we are willing to listen, to lead us into life.

My soul did trouble me

When the ego is troubled, it can be an anxious and fearful thing. But there is a different kind of troubling when the soul stirs us. A positively unsettling sense that we do not have to go with the inhuman flow, as Harry Eyres put it, but that we can walk a different path, a path less taken.

I love Susan Werner's song 'My Lord Did Trouble Me' (covered powerfully by Tom Jones on his album *Praise and Blame*), a song that is all about being troubled by God, who wants to awaken us from sleep. With 'a word' or 'a sign' or 'a ring of a bell at the back of my mind', the song goes, we can be troubled for the best reason possible – 'for to make me human, to make me whole'.

I wonder how you have felt troubled in a soulful way. Troubled enough, perhaps, to *do something* like turning the tables of the money-lenders, as Jesus did in the Temple in Jerusalem, when he could see that a 'house of prayer' had been turned into a place of corruption, 'a den of robbers'. It was a brave, fierce and sacrificial act that made him enemies.

*   *   *

We live in perilous times, and we should indeed be troubled: climate change, global inequality, over-population, mass migration, human conflict, economic collapse, the continued threat of terror and of religious fundamentalism . . . You name it, we seem to be handing it on to the next generation.

It can seem so hard to feel that we are able to make any kind of personal difference when the world is in such a state, so it's understandable that we may be so driven to distraction that we turn to shopping or TV, or become paralysed by fear to do nothing.

As Marilynne Robinson implies, however, if there is to be hope, then we must wake up to the way our egos collectively and individually compete, control and endlessly compare, and to the way we mindlessly sleep-walk through life, to re-awaken to the life beyond ego, which is where the adventure of soul begins.

It requires courageous people to set off on that adventure, in order for others to see their example and follow. But we can all be leaders, for it requires that each of us enters the pioneer territory of our own inner life – to reach further in – in order that we can reach further out to the world around us, in love.

I become a soulful leader when I learn to follow the leading of the soul. And this leading often comes in unexpected and unbidden ways . . .

*　　*　　*

I needed to pop out on foot (to buy a ticket from the station for a journey later that day). So I asked Betsy-Joy, my then three-year-old, if she fancied coming along. She was thrilled at the prospect of going for a wander.

As we set off – and it pains me to write this: how many times each day do we need reminding of the basics? – I became lost in thought almost immediately. Probably wondering what I'd write today. And pretty well the only thing I was conscious of was the tugging at my arm as I dragged my daughter along.

She was having a wander; I was trying to get some-where (physically and mentally). But as we drew nearer to the station, I experienced something akin to waking literally from a sleep. I could hear a voice, coming into sharper focus, speaking two words over and over, until I woke up fully and could hear them clearly:

'Daddy: moss!'

And there, growing on a low, dark and rather miss-able wall, were clumps of bright, soft moss. I stopped. And I said, 'Sorry.' As I knelt down, I could see that this low wall was high for her, and that she was seeing a very different world from down there. The clumps that were growing unmissably at her level made for a vivid sight, and we spent a while stroking the moss, feeling it, picking at it, even throwing it. And it was good.

It's funny what you can miss. As I looked with fresh eyes at the once-familiar pathway, she showed me other things I've never seen before, like an old window, way up high, and some words that had been scratched onto the wall nearby:

All that is gold does not glitter,
Not all those who wander are lost.

Indeed, indeed. All of which makes me wonder whether we can awaken today, to the tugging at our arm, and to the voice that is calling up to us, waking us as if from sleep.

*   *   *

Betsy-Joy was leading me as my soul wants to lead me, I do believe.

I was reminded, as I pondered this moment of awakening, of the words of Jesus, who said that you cannot enter the kingdom of heaven (by which I understand him to mean life in its fullness) 'unless you change and become like little children'.

He wasn't being nostalgic for that lost time of innocence when we were most fully present to the world set before us. He wasn't being nostalgic for an imagined yet forever out-of-reach state of spiritual perfection.

He was saying, I believe, that life in its fullness remains compellingly within reach, like a hand-hold, if we awaken to the tugging on the arm of our soul, and we stop, and open our eyes, and fall to our knees, and become like that child once more.

*   *   *

Here's one very simple exercise that I love to do from time to time, to remind me that I enter life most fully in a child-like way. And that's to try to see the world through the eyes of a child once more.

One way is to get down on the floor. Look at the room you are in from the perspective of a child. See through fresh eyes. What does this world you've become so used to look like through the wondering eyes of a child? What might you see from down there that you otherwise would not have spotted? Take time, just to take it all in, and let it speak to you.

You might also like, if you are able, to spend time with a child, and instead of telling them what to do, let them speak, let them act, watch and listen, and notice through their eyes what otherwise you would have missed.

* * *

I don't want to become a spiritual super-hero any more. I don't think I have it in me to become a Zen master. But I do want to live within the mystery and beauty of the soul's leading. I'm inspired by some of the 'greats' of art and literature and spirituality such as John O'Donohue who point to a different way of thinking and being. But just as significantly, I'm lifted by some of the greats within the ordinariness and pain of it all, who have connected daringly, differently. Like Linda. Or Howard. Or Heather. I expect you know some for yourself. And when I next see a rainbow, I will think of

them and remember that soulfulness is always within
reach.

> We *can* reach in, for soul,
> to meet our self, as if for the first time, and gain new
>   confidence in who we are.
> We can learn to see life differently, through the eyes
>   of the soul,
> and tap a wisdom that flows up from deeper in.

> We *can* reach out, through soul, to the world
>   around us,
> to reconnect with all parts of life, intuitively,
>   mindfully.
> We can seek soul friendship with God,
> go deeper with our friends and colleagues and family;
> even our enemies.
> We can rekindle our relationship with nature,
> and touch the world through love.

> We *can* embody this unique soul of ours, through
>   how and who we are,
> and what we do.
> We can seek out new rhythms;
> find a source of restoration, draw from the well
>   within.
> We can work with freedom and creativity;
> and see that we are indeed a part of the beauty of
>   all life;

We can make space for what really matters;
and the kind of space around us that gives others
the room to breathe again.
We may not be perfect, but we *are* whole; and by
embracing even the most difficult of situations,
we can be transformed. We *can*.

Epilogue: 'It is well with my soul'

In 1871, a prosperous lawyer called Horatio Spafford was living with his wife Anna, and their four young daughters in Lake View, Chicago. That year, a huge fire devastated the city, and for the following two years Horatio and Anna devoted their time to helping refugees from the fire who had been left with nothing.

By November 1873 the Spaffords needed respite and decided to join friends in Europe – but just before their departure Horatio was detained on business. He encouraged Anna and their four daughters to set off without him, but *en route* tragedy struck. The steamship they were travelling on, the *Ville de Havre*, sank after colliding with another ship in the middle of the ocean.

Out of the hundreds on board, Anna was one of only twenty-seven who were rescued, having been kept afloat by a piece of debris. Her daughters did not survive. In Chicago, Horatio received a tragic telegram from his wife, which read simply: 'Saved alone.'

Setting off to bring Anna home, he crossed the Atlantic, and mid-ocean, the captain of his vessel let him know that they were passing the approximate point where his daughters had died. He sat down and began to write the classic hymn which is still sung, and well loved, today, and contains the astonishing and moving words 'It is well with my soul'.

When peace, like a river, attendeth my way,
When sorrows like sea billows roll,
Whatever my lot, Thou has taught me to say,
It is well, it is well with my soul.
It is well, it is well with my soul.

Sometimes we receive the most beautiful yet fleeting moments of awakening, such as the appearance of a rainbow, that can touch our soul and remind us that there is more to life than this.

And sometimes we are stripped of everything. All goes dark.

Like the deepest of plantings.

No need to look enviously upon those who seem to have it all in this life – the trappings, the material comforts, the status – for what does it profit us to gain the whole world but lose our soul? This world was never ours to take in the first place. Our place, if you like, is within it, a part of the beauty, a part of the light and dark, earthed and expressed uniquely in love; to live as people who are unafraid to reach deeply in and to discover a soul friendship at the heart of all life that links us into the infinite, whether we like it or not, and will not let us rest happily in our mediocrity or escapism.

It was Horatio Spafford's love for God, and his awareness of God's love for him, that anchored him in even that most terrible of storms. I pray that whatever your circumstances, whatever you believe, and wherever you find yourself, you are able to say, like him, 'It is well with my soul.'

If you were to do one thing as a result of reading this book, what would it be?

So here we go. Either this book is filed on the shelves of your life as a (hopefully) stimulating and fascinating read, or ... it helps you to be transformed. Of course, the book itself will not transform you: only *you* can take the necessary steps to act decisively upon what you have read and do something about it.

But let me provide one suggestion, and (more importantly) a handful of questions. If you are serious about reaching further in, to reach out in love, then please take a few minutes, when next you have them, to enter your room, and close the door, and ask yourself the following:

- Which idea, in particular, has resonated most powerfully with me?
- Which practical exercise has had the most long-lasting effect so far?

- Which haven't I tried yet, that I still intend to?
- If I were to choose one thing to do differently, starting today for twenty-one days in order to form a habit, which would it be?
- What is most likely to stop me doing that?
- What difference would it make to me, and to those around me, if I were indeed to make it happen?
- What, then, *will* I do?

Seek and you will find

I really do believe that the soulful life is within reach, because we don't have to become perfect before we discover it. Be free from that burden!

And I simply refuse to believe that the God who is Love places all the riches that we yearn for – not ego-driven riches, but the riches of soul – agonisingly out of reach. Jesus said, 'Seek and you will find.' We may not always find what we thought we might – but from unexpected gifts hidden in plain sight, to the stretch of a soulful goal that, through intentional and mindful practice we might achieve, everything we need for the soulful life is within reach.

A friend asked me if I could sum up, very simply, what I do practically beyond all else, if I want to keep the channel open and stay soulfully connected to myself, and to God, and to creation.

My answer, for what it's worth, is this:

Get outside, often.
Slow your pace.
Breathe deeply.
Smile.
And keep watch.

Perhaps you will find a better way.
But whichever way you go:
Go *well*.

A reminder of the exercises and suggestions contained within this book

Part 1: What's right with mindfulness? An appreciative enquiry

- Sit quietly, and breathe.
- Make a cup of tea slowly, and make space to drink it, savouring it sip by sip.
- Become passionately absorbed in something you enjoy: build some Lego, bake a cake, chop some wood, stare out to sea, do some intricate colouring in, and don't feel guilty.
- Keep watch for the ideas that come from left-field; honour them when they arrive!
- Transform a journey: enjoy waiting at traffic lights, notice what you hear, what you see, how you feel. You are here, after all.
- Set your alarm for a few times throughout the day,

to remind you to stay wakeful with open-hearted presence.

- Give your attention to what you are doing, whether that's a complicated task at work, or the washing-up.
- Be kind – to yourself. You don't have to be perfect. Stop judging; give yourself a break.
- Count ten breaths. It doesn't take long, but it opens up powerful space within you and around you.
- Perform the miracle of walking the Earth. Take it slow. You have more time than you think.
- Find a journal that will inspire you to use it, and keep it with you, and write, doodle, draw, cut, paste, draw, dream!
- Do one thing at a time, and then the next. Be liberated from the panic of task switching.
- Savour the peace that comes with a quieter mind, and sense the presence of your soul waiting patiently beyond it.

Part 2: Reaching in for soul: awakening to our unique, inner aliveness

- Experience the sheer joy of being soul, not ego!
- Open your eyes and look *from* your soul; watch with love and compassion.
- Use soft eyes to see differently; to settle into the moment, to be 'here', and not to judge.

- Activate your senses: smell, taste, touch, look, hear . . . and tune back in to the world around you, lovingly. Let the taste of fruit, or the smell of coffee, or the sound of the rushing wind reconnect you with life!
- Collect those fleeting encounters that speak to you of a different narrative – those moments of serendipity or synchronicity. A stranger giving you bread to feed the ducks. Pay attention to them. Notice any trends or voices emerging, and let them speak!
- Give a stranger some bread to feed the ducks.
- Listen patiently and deeply to someone, tuning in lovingly, attentively. Try to hear something beyond their words.
- Listen to a piece of music as carefully as you did to that person. Tune in to it. Let it speak beyond the notes.
- Go back to your favourite soulful location, literally or in your mind, and let it touch you in the way that only it can.
- Step into a landscape and know that you are part of the beauty, not just a witness to it.
- See yourself as part of the hidden beauty of somewhere seemingly ugly.
- Wish yourself well: *May I be well, may I be peaceful, may I be happy, may I be loved.*
- Wish someone else well, whether a friend or enemy.

- Notice the times you do not act from your ego, and see what happens when soul takes a lead.
- Call your name, over and over, and be open to the 'more' of who you are. (When *did* you last meet yourself?)
- Consider the smallest details of someone you love, and tell them what you appreciate, and thank them for their soulfulness.
- Choose your funeral song. Listen to it. Imagine others listening too. Let it speak afresh of who you are and what you love.
- Reflect upon the emotions of your day, and where these took you.
- Watch for the unexpected tears, and pay close attention to what they might be saying and to where they might be leading. Sit with them, honour them, do not rush away from them.

Part 3: Reaching out with soul: reconnecting lovingly with all parts of life

- Make time to accept and receive the love of a soul friend.
- Enjoy someone's presence without cramming the space between you with words; savour stillness and be willing to sit in silence.
- Don't defend yourself, but allow yourself to be positively vulnerable.
- Look for God in the face of a stranger.

- Watch for God when you look in the mirror.
- Make space to sense more of the soul friendship of God.
- Step outside, into nature, and see what comes your way.
- Leave your camera or phone behind, and experience beauty without capturing it.
- Watch for rainbows, or kingfishers, or other fleeting natural features which reconnect you; let them come, and let them go, but feel their touch remaining.
- Take a slow walk beside a river just to be with it.
- Look for signs of nature in even the most urban of environments; hunt for flowers in the cracks of the concrete paving.
- Light a fire and watch the stars and invite others to share the experience.
- Spend time in a garden or allotment. Get soil in your fingernails. Cultivate your relationship with the earth – grow a plant from seed.
- Listen for birdsong and breathe the larger air.
- Celebrate the equinoxes and the solstices with a walk into the light and the dark.
- Watch clouds with a sense of joyful freedom.
- Stand by a tree and feel rooted.
- Step off the street into 'soul space' – into a church or a gallery.
- Visit your favourite café and ask why it inspires you.

- Tend to the space in which you live and work.
- Create an inspiring sense of soul space through your own presence.

Part 4: Living with soul: giving flesh-and-blood expression to the soulful life

- Perform a small and insignificant task in the way you would like to live the whole of your life.
- Create a *hygge*-like space and invite others into it; light candles, bake bread, make it welcoming. (Host a power cut evening, where you turn off the electricity.)
- Embrace the feelings you normally push away, through 'welcoming prayer'.
- Hug someone eight times in a day.
- Hug eight people in a day!
- Give yourself to the day instead of trying to take from it.
- Welcome the paradoxes at the heart of your life.
- Step out for a few minutes after dark to watch the moon; observe a cycle of the moon for a month, in this way, and reflect on the dark and light in your life; invite others you know from around the world to do this during the same cycle, as a way of expressing soulful contact at a distance.
- Experiment with finding a rhythm that works well for you, involving healthy habits of renewal and performance. (Give yourself a break: regularly.

Work in focused 'sprints'. Eat well. Drink water. Quit while you're ahead. Get some sleep. Make your sleeping space restful. Review your day with gratitude. Exercise! Go forest bathing.)

- Trace the source of a river or stream, and reflect on where you find the source of energy, wisdom and love in your own life.
- Savour the goodness of food or drink by pausing to breathe first. Invite others to eat with you.
- Receive from others with thanks!
- Start what you do from a place of contentment.
- Read a poem that inspires you.
- Be brave enough to express yourself creatively.
- Write a poem and then destroy it.
- Listen for a lark's song (or to Vaughan Williams's *The Lark Ascending*).
- Make visible what, without you, might never be seen.
- Let the beauty of what you love be what you do – take a risk to do what you love.
- Do something truly practical for someone else; don't just think about it, turn a great idea into action.
- Trust yourself next time you step out of your comfort zone.
- Embrace the unexpected and look for where it might lead you.
- Let your soul trouble you positively – 'with a word or a sign . . . or the ringing of a bell at the back of [your] mind'.

- Feel the tug of soul at your arm; sense its leading, and act upon it.
- Try to see the world through the eyes of a child.
- Honour someone who has inspired you.
- Inspire someone yourself.
- Make another cup of tea, slowly. And enjoy . . .

Acknowledgments

Thank you, Katherine Venn, for the love, care and soulful energy you brought to this project as its editor and originator. And for calling out the best in me.

Thank you, Heather and Dave Pearson, for your overflowing kindness.

Thank you, Luke and Jo Birmingham, for your enduring hospitality, which restoreth my soul.

Thank you, Alison Coulter and Nick Chatrath, for being soul partners in the business space.

Thank you, all who have been part of the 'Order of the Flower', who've met in the soul space we've shared on Friday nights around the kitchen table.

Thank you, Kats, for everything you poured into this this book yourself. You are my soul mate.

And thank you Eden, Mercy and Betsy-Joy for showing me the moss, and so much more.

Notes

p.ix   *A Hidden Wholeness: The Journey Toward an Undivided Life* (Jossey Bass, 2004), p. 16.

p.5   Mark 8.36.

p.7   See John 10.10.

pp.18–19   *Wherever You Go, There You Are: Mindfulness Meditations for Everyday Life* (Piatkus, 1994), p. 273.

p.21   http://www.oxfordmindfulness.org/about-mindfulness/

p.32   Psalm 46.10.

p.34   Adapted from Richard Rohr, *Breathing Under Water: Spirituality and the Twelve Steps* (Franciscan Media, 2011), pp. 84–7.

p.34   Proverbs 20.5 (TM).

p.41   http://www.mindful.org/five-steps-to-mindfulness/

p.49   *Soulcraft: Crossing into the Mysteries of Nature and Psyche* (New World Library, 2010), p. 37.

p.53   John 5.6.

p.55   Romans 12.2.

p.59   Psalm 139.14.

p.65 *Life After God* (Washington Square Press, 1995).

p.66 *Anam Cara: Spiritual Wisdom from the Celtic World* (Bantam Press, 1997), p.40.

p.67 Quote from an article about Macdonald in *The British Friend Journal*, 1892; more about this from William O'Flaherty, http://www.essentialcslewis.com/2015/10/17/are-a-soul/

p.68 J.K. Chamblin, 'Psychology', in *Dictionary of Paul and His Letters*, ed. G.F. Hawthorne, R.P. Martin and D.G. Reid (IVP, 1993), p. 765.

p.70 See, for instance, *Immortal Diamond: The Search for our True Self* (SPCK, 2013).

p.70 Genesis 1.31.

p.72 Eckhart Tolle, *The Power of Now: A Guide to Spiritual Enlightenment* (New World Library, 1999; repr. Hodder Mobius, 2001), pp. 14–15.

p.75 Psalm 42.7.

p.78 Rod Windle and Suzanne Warren, *Collaborative Problem Solving and Dispute Resolution in Special Education*, http://www.directionservice.org/cadre/forward.cfm

p.81 Material drawn from *Just Listen!* – a DVD produced by Acorn Christian Healing Foundation, http://www.acornchristian.org

p.92 Loving-kindness meditation by Kathleen Grace-Bishop: https://www.youtube.com/watch?v=sz7cpV7ERsM

p.94 Matthew 5.44.

pp.100–101 Matthew 26.29.

p.101 Isaiah 65.17; 2 Peter 3.13; Revelation 21.1.

p.101 John 21.

p.107 *Reimagining the Ignatian Examen: Fresh Ways to Pray from Your Day* (Loyola Press, 2015).

p.108 *Whistling in the Dark: A Doubter's Dictionary* (Harper SanFrancisco, 1993 – first published 1988).

p.109 Matthew 13.3–8.

p.120 *Falling Upward: A Spirituality for the Two Halves of Life* (Jossey Bass, 2011), p. 91.

p.121 Colossians 1.27

p.123 Psalm 62.5. (ESV).

p.123 Matthew 6.6.

p.124–5 Psalm 139.

p.125 1 John 4.8.

p.126 *Reclaiming the Wild Soul: How Earth's Landscapes Restore Us to Wholeness* (White Cloud Press, 2014).

p.136 *The South Country* (Nature Classics Library; Little Toller Books, 2009).

p.137 Julie Moir Messervy, *The Inward Garden: Creating a Place of Beauty and Meaning* (Bunker Hill Publishing, 2007).

p.138 'Gardening Work', from *The Soul of Rumi: A New Collection of Ecstatic Poems*, compiled by Colman Barks (HarperOne, 2001).

p.141 'Cloudy With a Chance of Joy', TED Talk, TED Global, June 2013; https://www.ted.com/talks/gavin_pretor_pinney_cloudy_with_a_chance_of_joy?language=en

p.142 *Naked Spirituality: A Life with God in Twelve Simple Words* (Hodder & Stoughton, 2011).

p.143 *Christ Plays in Ten Thousand Places: A Conversation in Spiritual Theology* (Hachette UK, 2011).

p.143 1 Corinthians 13.4–8.

pp.146–7 'This Column Will Change Your Life: Where Heaven and Earth Collide' (*Observer*, 22 March 2014); http://www.theguardian.com/lifeandstyle/2014/mar/22/this-column-change-your-life-heaven-earth

p.158 Matthew 20.16.

p.163 Megan Hickey, 'Is the Secret of Happiness Contained in this Danish Word?' *PBS News Hour*; http://www.pbs.org/newshour/updates/key-work-life-balance-contained-danish-word/

p.168 '4 Benefits of Hugs, For Mind and Body, Psychology Today' (Blog); https://www.psychologytoday.com/blog/unified-theory-happiness/201406/4-benefits-hugs-mind-and-body

p.169 Paul Zak, 'Trust, Morality – and Oxytocin?', TEDGlobal 2011; https://www.ted.com/talks/paul_zak_trust_morality_and_oxytocin?language=en

p.169 Luke 15.11–32.

p.184 https://mobile.twitter.com/christinecaine/status/571814033780682752

p.186 *Learning to Walk in the Dark* (Canterbury Press, 2014).

p.188 Anne Lamott, *Stitches: A Handbook on Meaning, Hope and Repair* (Hodder & Stoughton, 2014).

p.190 Maya Angelou, Facebook page: https://www.facebook.com/MayaAngelou/posts/10150251846629796

p.191 Tony Schwartz, with Jean Gomes and Catherine McCarthy, *The Way We're Working Isn't Working: The Four Forgotten Needs that Energize Great Performance* (Simon & Schuster, 2010), p. 57.

p.201 Robert Penn, 'Mood Enhancer: Go Down to the Woods Today' – article in the *Observer*, Sunday 25 October 2015; http://www.theguardian.com/life-andstyle/2015/oct/25/mood-enhancer-go-down-to-the-woods-today-depression

p.202 Matthew 4.4; Jesus was quoting Deuteronomy 8.3.

p.205 Psalm 42.1.

p.208 Matthew 6:25, 34.

p.212 Robert Bresson, *Notes on the Cinematographer* (Sun and Moon Classics; Green Integer, 2009).

p.218 *The Essential Rumi*, trans. Coleman Barks with John Moyne (1995).

p.219 'Walking the Mystical Path with Practical Feet' (a talk presented at the Institute of Noetic Sciences conference, 2001, Palm Springs, CA).

p.220 Cynthia Bourgeault, *The Wisdom Way of Knowing: Reclaiming an Ancient Tradition to Awaken the Heart* (Jossey Bass, 2003).

p.223 Otto Scharmer and Katrin Kaufer, *Leading from the Emerging Future: From Ego-system to Eco-system Economies* (Berrett-Koehler, 2013).

p.224 Frederic Laloux, *Reinventing Organizations: A Guide to Creating Human Organizations Inspired by the Next Stage of Human Consciousness* (Nelson Parker, 2014).

pp.228–9 Harry Eyres, 'Getting & Spending', in the *Independent* magazine, 24 October 2015, p. 33.

p.230 Matthew 21:13.

p.233 Matthew 18:3.

p.242 Matthew 7.7.

BE STILL and KNOW that I AM GOD

PSALM 46:10

The Heavens & the Earth
Stu McLellan

ISBN: 9781473637337

If you'd like to do some soulful meditation on a whole
range of words from the Bible (some of which feature
in this book), this beautiful new colouring book by
Stu McLellan will engage your mind and soul.

Do you wish this wasn't the end?
Are you hungry for more great teaching, inspiring
testimonies, ideas to challenge your faith?

Join us at www.hodderfaith.com, follow us on Twitter
or find us on Facebook to make sure you get the latest from
your favourite authors.

Including interviews, videos, articles, competitions
and opportunities to tell us just what you thought about
our latest releases.

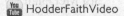
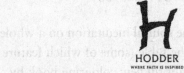